To Garre

FoR

& maturity as

of The Christ

John Copper

RMTDW #31

Sept. '21

MW01282102

THE DILIGENCE OF DISCIPLESHIP

Preparing for Glory

JOHN A. COPPER

WESTBOW
PRESS®
A DIVISION OF THOMAS NELSON
& ZONDERVAN

WestBow Press books may be ordered through booksellers or by contacting:

WestBow Press
A Division of Thomas Nelson & Zondervan
1663 Liberty Drive
Bloomington, IN 47403
www.westbowpress.com
1 (866) 928-1240

ISBN: 978-1-9736-8732-0 (sc)
ISBN: 978-1-9736-8731-3 (hc)
ISBN: 978-1-9736-8733-7 (e)

Library of Congress Control Number: 2020903861

Print information available on the last page.

WestBow Press rev. date: 03/06/2020

CONTENTS

To my *Kephzibah*
My delight is in her.
And to the
Saints of Surface Creek Community Church.

They have borne with great patience my
deliberations for this book.
Thank you.

PREFACE

I have observed in thirty-plus years of pulpit ministry that there is a weakness in the process of discipleship in the church of Jesus Christ. This book is not primarily about showing that weakness. Rather, I define biblical discipleship and provide a simple-to-grasp but difficult-to-do five-step process to transforming converts into maturing disciples of Jesus Christ.

While this is not a book on Bible doctrine, it will be helpful to understand my doctrinal basis and bias. I grew up in a fundamental Baptist church and earned my degrees in biblical studies and theology from a biblically conservative Baptist Bible college. During the last twenty-plus years I have studied various schools of theology, especially Dispensational, Messianic, Orthodox, and Reformed. Mostly, I adhere to Reformed theology, expressed in the doctrines of grace. I believe the biblical doctrine of salvation by grace alone, through faith alone, and that works of righteousness have no merit for salvation but proceed from salvation:

> For by grace you are saved through faith, and
> this is not from yourselves, it is the gift of God; it

is not from works, so that no one can boast. For we are his creative work, having been created in Christ Jesus for good works that God prepared beforehand so we can do them. (Eph 2:8–10)

I believe in the perseverance of the saints, that all who are born again will surely be saved, and that Jesus will lose nothing of all that has been given Him:

Now this is the will of the one who sent me—that I should not lose one person of every one he has given me, but raise them all up at the last day. For this is the will of my Father—for everyone who looks on the Son and believes in him to have eternal life, and I will raise him up at the last day. (Jn 6:39–40)

It is not within the purview of this book to defend these doctrines; there are many books, both ancient and modern, that the reader could consult. However, it will be important to remember these doctrines as you progress through this study.

I am concerned for the welfare of the church. The church is composed of individuals, thus I am concerned for your welfare. My concern stems from three separate but related teachings of Jesus and an ominous warning. These teachings and the warning are not primarily for those outside the church but for those who inhabit the church. I will state them briefly here. I encourage the reader to meditate more fully on them.

First, the parable of the sower:

On that day after Jesus went out of the house, he sat by the lake. And such a large crowd gathered around him that he got into a boat to sit while the whole crowd stood on the shore. He told them many things in parables, saying: "Listen! A sower went out to sow. And as he sowed, some seeds fell along the path, and the birds came and devoured them. Other seeds fell on rocky ground where they did not have much soil. They sprang up quickly because the soil was not deep. But when the sun came up, they were scorched, and because they did not have sufficient root, they withered. Other seeds fell among the thorns, and they grew up and choked them. But other seeds fell on good soil and produced grain, some a hundred times as much, some sixty, and some thirty. The one who has ears had better listen! (Mt 13:1–9)

So listen to the parable of the sower: When anyone hears the word about the kingdom and does not understand it, the evil one comes and snatches what was sown in his heart; this is the seed sown along the path. The seed sown on rocky ground is the person who hears the word and immediately receives it with joy. But he has no root in himself and does not endure; when trouble or persecution comes because of the word, immediately he falls away. The seed sown among thorns is the person who hears the word, but worldly cares and the seductiveness of wealth choke the word, so it produces nothing. But as for the seed sown on good soil, this is the person who hears the word and understands. He bears fruit, yielding a hundred, sixty, or thirty times what was sown. (Mt 13:18–23)

Forgetting the chapter divisions and the section headings, notice this parable follows directly after a statement by Jesus in which He distinguishes who "is my brother and sister and mother": "For whoever does the will of my Father in heaven is my brother and sister and mother" (Mt 12:50). He states that obedience to the will of His Father supersedes blood relationship. The parable of the sower follows immediately (13:3–9), with the explanation by Jesus following that (13:18–23). The seed is the word of the kingdom (13:18, 20, 21, 23). The soil is the heart of those who hear the Word. Jesus used metaphors of "the path", the "rocky ground", "among thorns", and "good soil" to describe the hearts.

The Father is looking for a harvest; the seed on the path does not even crack or sprout but is consumed by the evil one; the seed on the rocky ground does not establish roots, so it perishes in the sun's heat; the seed among thorns has the opportunity to produce a harvest but is choked out by the thorns; the seed scattered in the good soil produces the harvest the Father is looking for, some a hundredfold, some sixty, some thirty. In each case, the failure or the harvest is not determined by the quality of the seed but by the receptivity of the soil. Obviously, the Father is looking for the seeds that bear fruit (v. 23). It behooves us, therefore, to condition our hearts to bear fruit, the fruit of the Spirit:

> But the fruit of the Spirit is love, joy, peace, patience, kindness, goodness, faithfulness, gentleness, and self-control. Against such things there is no law. Now those who belong to Christ have crucified the flesh with its passions and desires. If we live by the Spirit, let us also behave in accordance with the Spirit. (Gal 5:22–25)

This is what the Father expects. The true goal of each individual Christian is, or should be, to break up the fallow ground, to cultivate their heart, that the Lord may come and rain righteousness upon them: "Yes, this is what the LORD has said to the people of Judah and Jerusalem: 'Break up your unplowed ground, do not cast seeds among thorns'" (Jer 4:3); and "Sow righteousness for yourselves, reap unfailing love. Break up the unplowed ground for yourselves, for it is time to seek the LORD, until he comes and showers deliverance on you" (Hos 10:12).

Second, the parable of the weeds, or the wheat and the tares:

> He presented them with another parable: "The kingdom of heaven is like a person who sowed good seed in his field. But while everyone was sleeping, an enemy came and sowed darnel among the wheat and went away. When the plants sprouted and produced grain, then the darnel also

appeared. So the slaves of the landowner came and said to him, 'Sir, didn't you sow good seed in your field? Then where did the darnel come from?' He said, 'An enemy has done this!' So the slaves replied, 'Do you want us to go and gather it?' But he said, 'No, since in gathering the darnel you may uproot the wheat along with it. Let both grow together until the harvest. At harvest time I will tell the reapers, "First collect the darnel and tie it in bundles to be burned, but then gather the wheat into my barn."'" (Mt 13:24–30)

Then he left the crowds and went into the house. And his disciples came to him saying, "Explain to us the parable of the darnel in the field." He answered, "The one who sowed the good seed is the Son of Man. The field is the world and the good seed are the people of the kingdom. The poisonous weeds are the people of the evil one, and the enemy who sows them is the devil. The harvest is the end of the age, and the reapers are angels. As the poisonous weeds are collected and burned with fire, so it will be at the end of the age. (Mt 13:36–40)

In this parable, the Son of Man (Jesus) plants good seed (sons of the kingdom) in the world. But Satan, the enemy of the Son of Man, plants weeds who are the sons of the evil one in the field (the world). In this parable, the sons of the kingdom are hard to discern from the sons of the evil one because the evil one has planted seeds that bear a resemblance to those planted by the Son of Man. Though they bear a resemblance, the fruit of the evil one is destructive, not life-giving as is the fruit of the Son of Man. God has warned the sons of the kingdom about false prophets and false teachers since the beginning, and Satan is the father of lies (Jn 8:44). In the theology of the Jews, there are two ages—this present age and the age to come, the Messianic age. At the end of this present age,

> The Son of Man will send his angels, and they will gather out of his kingdom all causes of sin and all law-breakers, and throw them into the fiery furnace. In that place there will be weeping and gnashing of teeth. (Mt 13:41–42 ESV)

Following this cosmic weeding, "the righteous will shine like the sun in the kingdom of their Father. He who has ears, let him hear" (Mt 13:43 ESV). God distinguishes between His own seeds and the seeds of the evil one. To the untrained eye, sometimes they appear to be indistinguishable, but the Father knows. How does He know? He knows by the "grain" (v. 26). Here again, the fruit is the distinguishing characteristic. What distinguishes you from the world, dear reader?

Third, the vine, the branches, the fruit, and the glory of the Father:

> I am the true vine, and my Father is the vinedresser. Every branch in me that does not bear fruit he

takes away, and every branch that does bear fruit he prunes, that it may bear more fruit. Already you are clean because of the word that I have spoken to you. Abide in me, and I in you. As the branch cannot bear fruit by itself, unless it abides in the vine, neither can you, unless you abide in me. I am the vine; you are the branches. Whoever abides in me and I in him, he it is that bears much fruit, for apart from me you can do nothing. If anyone does not abide in me he is thrown away like a branch and withers; and the branches are gathered, thrown into the fire, and burned. If you abide in me, and my words abide in you, ask whatever you wish, and it will be done for you. By this my Father is glorified, that you bear much fruit and so prove to be my disciples. (Jn 15:1–8 ESV)

In this third teaching, Jesus is alone with His disciples on the night before He is crucified. He knows of His impending death. He tells His disciples the most important things. In this illustration, Jesus is the Vine; individuals who claim to be "in Christ" are the branches. What the vinedresser, the Father, is looking for is fruit, the fruit of the Spirit (Gal 5:22–24). As the vinedresser examines the branches, He notes those that do not produce the desired fruit, and He takes them away. He prunes those that produce the blessed fruit so they might produce even more. Those taken away are gathered, thrown into the fire, and burned (v. 6). The branch has no capacity to bear fruit in and of itself; the branch produces fruit as it *abides* in the Vine. To abide is to remain in the Vine in such a way as to draw the life source from the Vine (v. 4). Then Jesus tells the disciples plainly, "By this my Father is glorified, that you bear much fruit and so prove to be my disciples" (Jn 15:8 ESV). If we live to glorify God, and we should, then we *must* bear fruit; it is in bearing fruit we *prove* we are His. In verse 7, the granting of our prayers will glorify the Father, and in that, we will be fruitful and so become, or prove that we are, His disciples. A disciple with no fruit is not a disciple; it is a useless branch to be taken away and thrown into the fire.

The fourth and final teaching considered here is toward the close of the Sermon on the Mount as recorded by Matthew. It is helpful to read Matthew chapter 7 without the section headings. The message is easily broken up and misconstrued by them. Contrary to popular opinion, this chapter does not teach that we are not "to judge." It teaches us how to make accurate judgments through discernment and wisdom. Often the criteria for making judgments or discernments are through observation of the fruit:

> Watch out for false prophets, who come to you in sheep's clothing but inwardly are voracious wolves. You will recognize them by their fruit. Grapes are not gathered from thorns or figs from thistles, are they? In the same way, every good tree bears good fruit, but the bad tree bears bad fruit. A good tree is not able to bear bad fruit, nor a bad tree to bear good fruit. Every tree that does

not bear good fruit is cut down and thrown into the fire. So then, you will recognize them by their fruit. (Mt 7:15–20)

False teachers and false prophets are recognized by their corrupt fruit; they cannot fit through the narrow gate:

Enter through the narrow gate, because the gate is wide and the way is spacious that leads to destruction, and there are many who enter through it. How narrow is the gate and difficult the way that leads to life, and there are few who find it! (Mt 7:13–14)

Ultimately, the Father will cast them out from His presence:

Not everyone who says to me, "Lord, Lord," will enter into the kingdom of heaven—only the one who does the will of my Father in heaven. On that day, many will say to me, "Lord, Lord, didn't we prophesy in your name, and cast out demons in your name, and do many powerful deeds in your name?" Then I will declare to them, "I never knew you. Go away from me, you lawbreakers!" (Mt 7:21–23)

Once again, it is the fruit of the Spirit that determines the eternal value and destination. The conclusion is in verses 24–27:

Everyone who hears these words of mine and does them is like a wise man who built his house on rock. The rain fell, the flood came, and the winds beat against that house, but it did not collapse because its foundation had been laid on rock. Everyone who hears these words of mine and does not do them is like a foolish man who built his house on sand. The rain fell, the flood came, and the winds beat against that house, and it collapsed—it was utterly destroyed!

To know the Word of God is not enough. Even if we can quote it extensively, we do not impress the Father. We must *do* the Word of God. This fourth teaching, especially verses 21–23, should be sufficiently terrifying to motivate us to be sure we have broken up the fallow ground for the seed; that our lives distinguish us from the world; that we are abiding in Christ, so stuck to Him we are producing good fruit; that we can rightly discern between the truth of the Father and false teachers and so build our house on the Rock.

The thrust of this book is to come alongside the Christian and offer a workable plan for bearing much fruit. The reader should not assume that to read through this book once will suffice. I encourage particular, repeated exposure to at least section 2, "The Process of Discipleship." Memorizing and practicing the five steps in this process will cause the fruit to begin to "grow and show."

In *The Diligence of Discipleship*, our goal is to glorify God in our lives. That is the goal of the Christian life, nothing more, nothing less, nothing else. We will learn some verses and processes to incorporate into our lives. I guarantee if you stick with this, if you take notes, if you do the homework, it will be the hardest exercise you have ever submitted yourself to. Ever. Why? Because we are talking about nothing less than the total transformation of who you are. But it will also be the most rewarding. Biblical discipleship is the opportunity to improve your relationship with the Father and your relationships with others.

It is said that God loves you just the way you are. But He loves you far too much to leave you that way. With all that God has done for us in redemption, there is yet much that remains for us to do in sanctification. Transforming who we are of necessity forces us to admit that we need to change. I have encouraged my students, as I have done myself, to attach a sticker to their mirror with this quote: "You are looking at the problem," and another sticker in their workplace with this quote: "You must participate in your own rescue." The first quote is from a former employer of mine and the second from a river-raft guide. I took the title of this series from 2 Peter 1:5; the New American Standard Bible reads "applying all diligence …" All diligence; the diligence of discipleship. It is your responsibility as a Christian to do the hard work of transformation to be a disciple of Jesus Christ. We will learn more about what that really means and how to do it. "A disciple is not greater than his teacher, but everyone when fully trained will be like his teacher" (Lk 6:40).

SECTION 1

CHAPTER 1

DEFINITIONS

Have you ever used a word without knowing what it meant? I have. It was embarrassing when someone brought it to my attention. Or have you ever read a book in which the author uses words you are not familiar with or words you have read before but are not sure what they mean? The theologian John Calvin is such an author for me; he uses words I am unfamiliar with. What exactly does "calumniate" mean? Sometimes I try to guess the meaning of an unfamiliar word from the context, but it is best for me to read his commentaries or his Institutes with a good dictionary in hand, a dictionary from that period, because the meaning of words are liable to change.

Then there are words we are familiar with, words we hear or read often enough, but perhaps we do not understand the depth of their meanings. We have only a vague idea of their meanings, although we think we have a good understanding of the word. When this is true, we are, in some measure, deceived, deceived by the words we use, not fully understanding their implications.

I believe there are words in the Bible that fit into this category. Either we do not know what they mean, or we have only a cursory understanding. Before making progress in *The Diligence of Discipleship*, there are five words we need to define in their biblical context. These words are *diligent, glory* or *glorify, follow* or *follower, disciple,* and *servant.* Without a proper understanding of these words, we cripple our discipleship. These definitions are a little long; the summaries are on pages 17-18.

Diligent

As mentioned in the preface, I took the title of this book from 2 Peter 1:5 (NASB), which states in part, "applying all diligence." The English Standard Version translates it as "make every effort." The Greek word used in this verse is *spoudē,* pronounced *spoo-day.* The English word *diligent* expresses the idea behind this Greek word. *Webster's Dictionary of American English* (1828) defines diligent, in part, as "constant in effort or exertion to accomplish what is undertaken." Thus, in 2 Peter 1:5, Peter exhorts the disciples to be constant in effort or exertion to accomplish what they undertake. And what they undertake is the formation of a godly character. Paul used a variant of this same Greek word in 2 Timothy 2:15, which the King James Version translates, "Study to shew thyself approved unto God." But as shown in this study, it requires much more than study; the disciple must be constant in effort or exertion to accomplish what he or she undertakes. Other translations render this as "Be diligent" (NASB, NKJV, HCSB) or "Do your best" (ESV). The diligent person is one who is not distracted. A world-class athlete is careful and persistent in his or her work or effort. For this study, we understand *diligence* or *diligent* as marked by careful and persistent work or effort.

Glory or Glorify

In questions related to idolatry, sexual immorality, and food sacrificed to idols, Paul offered this conclusion: "So whether you eat or drink, or whatever you do, do everything for the glory of God" (1 Cor 10:31). "Do everything for the glory of God." What exactly does that mean? The Greek word translated as "glory" is *doxa*. According to *The New International Dictionary of New Testament Theology* (NIDNTT), *doxa* and its various cognates "affords one of the clearest examples of change in meaning of a Gk. word, when it came under the influence of the Bible."[1] In the secular Greek of the classical period, the meaning of *doxa* is an opinion or conjecture, and it could imply repute, praise, or fame. Those who translated the Hebrew Old Testament (OT) into Greek (the Septuagint, or LXX) transformed the secular concept of doxa; we do not find that it is just an opinion.

> The meanings of praise and honor are shared with secular Gk. But whereas *doxa* is seldom used for the honour shown to a man ..., it is frequently used for the honor brought or given to God. ...

---

[1] S. Aalen, "Glory, Honour," In *The New International Dictionary of New Testament Theology*, ed. Colin Brown (Grand Rapids: Zondervan, 1980), 2:44.

But above all, *doxa* expresses God's glory and power.[2]

Doxa is found approximately 165 times in the New Testament (NT) in the context we are looking at (1 Cor 10:31), it means specifically honor, fame, and repute, or in the verb form, to honor or praise. According to Paul, all that we do should reflect this. When we leave a conversation or an event, we should enhance the reputation of God in the minds of those who have interacted with us. For this study "to do all to the glory of God" is to honor Him and to enhance His reputation among humankind.

Follow or Follower

If we are to understand our relationship to Jesus Christ, we must understand the biblical context of a follower. The Greek word most often associated with a follower of Jesus is *akoloutheō*, pronounced *ak-ol-oo-theh'-o*. It is formed from a word that, in the secular Greek of the classical period, means a path, and from that, it takes on the meaning to go somewhere, to go with someone, to pursue someone. Metaphorically, it came to mean to go along with someone's opinion, to follow or agree with another's opinion or argument. From this, the Stoics (an ancient Greek school of philosophy) gave akoloutheō religious and philosophical associations. Among them, "following here virtually means identification of one's being through incorporation. Behind this lies the Gk. view of the innate relationship of rational man with

---

[2] Aalen, "Glory, Honour," 2:44.

God."[3] It is important to understand how the Greeks used this word as it reflects on the Greek translation of the OT, the LXX.

While the Greeks under the Stoics were developing *following* as being the identification of one's being through incorporation, the Hebrews did not have this concept in their language. They understood humankind in relationship to God as obedient, never as becoming as God. However, after the return from Babylonian exile and the conquest of Alexander the Great, the Hebrew and Greek cultures began to mingle. When cultures mingle, language changes. During this period, we witness the emergence of rabbis, in some degree fashioned after the Greek philosophers who often had students gathered to them. Concerning the emergence of this relationship, the NIDNTT states:

> The words describe the relationship of a pupil to a teacher of the Torah. The pupil ... who chooses to subordinate himself to a Rabbi follows him everywhere he goes, learning from him and above all serving him. The pupil's obligation to serve is an essential part of learning the Law. The goal of all his learning and training is a complete knowledge of the Torah, and ability to practise it in every situation. Without this, true piety is scarcely deemed possible.[4]

---

[3] C. Blendinger, "Disciple, Follow, Imitate, After," In *The New International Dictionary of New Testament Theology*, ed. Colin Brown (Grand Rapids: Zondervan, 1980), 1:481.

[4] Blendinger, "Disciple, Follow, Imitate, After," 1:481.

The follower was as much a servant as a student contributing to the support of the rabbi. This was a new relationship in Judaism, not known to the fathers, and was brought in through the influence of the Greeks.

In the NT, the word *akoloutheō* occurs primarily in the Gospels, the writings nearest to the rabbinic world. Sometimes the word is used to describe those who follow Jesus, not from conviction, but from curiosity; I call them the curious onlookers (Mt 4:25; 8:1; 21:9). The rich young man, for example, was a curious onlooker.

> Jesus said to him, "If you wish to be perfect, go sell your possessions and give the money to the poor, and you will have treasure in heaven. Then come, follow me." But when the young man heard this he went away sorrowful, for he was very rich. (Mt 19:21–22)

Unlike the rabbis, Jesus called His followers individually. With rabbis, the followers sought the rabbi. Jesus would issue a command to "follow me," as in Matthew 9:9. He sought His followers, as evidenced with Philip: "On the next day Jesus wanted to set out for Galilee. He *found* Philip and said to him, 'Follow me'" (Jn 1:43; italics added). The call of Jesus to be a disciple is decisive, intimate, and effectual. He called with divine authority. The NIDNTT observes that "As a rule, the one who takes up the new 'calling' gives the old one up."[5] The author also notes that

---

[5] Blendinger, "Disciple, Follow, Imitate, After," 1:482.

Since the disciple cannot expect any better fortune than his Lord (cf. Matt. 10:24 f.), readiness for suffering becomes a part of discipleship. "If any man would come after me, let him deny himself and take up his cross and follow me" (Mk. 8:34; cf. Matt. 10:38). "To take up the cross" means "to be ready for death" (G. Delling, *TDNT* IV 6). But readiness to suffer is only made possible through the "self-denial" which consists in freedom from oneself and all forms of personal security. Such self-denial is possible only when man gives himself to God in unconditional discipleship.[6]

For this study, as the word is used by Jesus, to be a follower or to follow Jesus means the person has found "a new settled purpose as they are directed into the true life."[7]

Disciple

The follower of Jesus has a certain well-defined relationship to Jesus. The true disciple is, likewise, in a certain well-defined relationship to Jesus. I am not convinced that most who call themselves "disciples" of Christ have a very good understanding of the implication of that relationship. The Greek word most often associated with a disciple of Jesus is *mathētēs*, pronounced *math-ay-tes'*. In the secular Greek of the classical era, this word in the

---

[6] Blendinger. "Disciple, Follow, Imitate, After," 1:482-483.

[7] Blendinger. "Disciple, Follow, Imitate, After," 1:483.

noun form would describe a person who today we would call an apprentice. This person would attach himself or herself to another to learn or gain practical and/or theoretical knowledge; this could be in the trades, in medicine, or a learner in a school, particularly philosophy. Generally, the mathētēs had to pay a fee to the one who was the master or teacher (Gk. *didaskalos*).

In the history of Israel, before the captivity in Babylon, there was no relationship similar to the apprentice or mathētēs of the classical Greek era. The Hebrew people had a national identity beginning with the Exodus, in which each person was a learner, responsible to learn the Torah from Moses and later from the prophets and/or the priests. On this, the NIDNTT states,

> … the attendants of Moses and the prophets are not called pupils but servants. … Joshua is the servant of Moses (Exod. 24:12; Num. 11:28); Elisha is the servant of Elijah (1Ki. 19:19 ff.); Gehazi of Elisha (2Ki. 4:12); Baruch of Jeremiah (Jer. 32:12 f.).[8]

Each individual, as a learner, was absorbed into the national identity of an elect people, the people of God. There was no possibility of a master-disciple relationship between people because all—prophet, priest, and king—owed their allegiance to God and to God alone.

Returning from the Babylonian exile, under the leadership

---

[8] D. Müller, "Disciple, Follow, Imitate, After," In *The New International Dictionary of New Testament Theology*, ed. Colin Brown (Grand Rapids: Zondervan, 1980), 1:485.

of Ezra into the Rabbinic period and mingling with the Greek culture after Alexander the Great, the relationship of teacher-student takes on a distinctive Jewish flavor. Here, the Hebrew *talmid*, the early equivalent of the Greek *mathētēs*, "is someone whose concern is the whole of Jewish tradition."[9] During this time, the role of the rabbi gained increasing importance, while the talmid, or mathētēs, was in an almost servile relationship to the rabbi. The disciple was to learn the whole of both the written Torah (the OT), and the oral Torah (the traditions of the fathers); the rabbi stood between the disciple and the Torah, almost as a mediator. This developing relationship, built on achievement in religious thought, gave a value to human authority that was previously unknown in Judaism. This gave rise to a class of men without whose guidance the study of the scriptures was to be avoided at all costs. In this system "learning is determined by the authority of the teacher and his interpretation of the Torah—not by personal and, as far as possible, unbiased study of the Torah."[10]

With this value on human authority, and *talmidim* (students or learners) who completed their studies, the natural outgrowth, as in the Greek philosophical model, is the development of differing schools of thought or interpretation. Gone are the authoritative prophets, those who command authority directly from God; here, competing ideas are the norm, and with the increase in the numbers of rabbis, a corresponding decrease in the surety of "absolute truth." What began with Ezra as a teacher-student relationship became, through commingling the Jewish and Greek

---

[9] Müller, "Disciple, Follow, Imitate, After," 1:485.
[10] Müller. "Disciple, Follow, Imitate, After," 1:485.

cultures, the rabbi-talmid schools that dotted the landscape as Jesus entered the world.

In the NT, the Greek *mathētēs* appears, depending on the family of manuscripts used, either 264 or 268 times, and this only in the Gospels and Acts. "It is used to indicate total attachment to someone in discipleship."[11] Even as the word *mathētēs* in the rabbinic culture was heavily influenced by the Greek culture, in association with Jesus, it takes on a new character. Sometimes the evangelists used the word in relationships other than with Jesus. There are the disciples of John the Baptizer (Mt 11:2; Mk 2:18), the disciples of Moses (Jn 9:28), and the disciples of the Pharisees (Mt 22:16; Mk 2:18). The first two disciples of Jesus came from the disciples of John the Baptizer (Jn 1:25–40). Unlike the rabbinic schools, in which a man would seek and join a particular school, with Jesus it was uniquely His call that was decisive (Lk 5:1–11; Mk 1:17). In the rabbi-disciple relationship, they understood that the disciple wanted to become a master or rabbi, with all the attendant societal benefits. This was not true of the Jesus-disciple relationship. His disciples sought only to lead others to the Master, never to become a master themselves; death is the only graduation.

With Jesus, the call to discipleship means a call to service, not to be served (Mk 9:35); His disciples are to be "fishers of men" (Mt 4:19; Mk 1:17). This service could well lead to dangers and death, even as the Master was subject to dangers and death (Jn 15:18, 25). Jesus restored the pursuit of, and the reality of absolute truth. He said, "I am the way, and the truth, and the life. No one comes to

---

[11] Müller. "Disciple, Follow, Imitate, After," 1:486.

the Father except through me" (Jn 14:6). The disciple of Jesus has faith in Jesus and in Him alone (Jn 2:11; 6:69; 14:1); he does not pursue the acclaim of any other but gives himself wholly to Jesus and in service wholly to Jesus. For this study,

> *Following Jesus as a disciple means the unconditional sacrifice of his whole life* (Matt. 10:37; Lk. 14:26 f.; cf. Mk. 3:31–35; Lk. 9:59–62) *for the whole of his life* (Matt. 10:24 ff.; Jn. 11:16). *To be a disciple means* (as Matt. in particular emphasizes) *to be bound to Jesus and to do God's will* (Matt. 12:46–50; cf. Mk. 3:31–35).[12] (emphasis mine)

Servant

We learned in the previous words *follower* and *disciple* that the Christian has a well-defined relationship to Jesus. Another dimension in that relationship is revealed in the term variously translated as "servant," "slave," "bondslave," and "bond-servants." I believe this biblical term is not well understood in the Western church primarily because of our limited acquaintance with actual servanthood and slavery. While the practice of slavery existed in our history, the fact is that few people alive today in the United States and in Europe experienced the relationship of slavery or servanthood. Biblically, Israel, the descendants of Jacob, have a long history of slavery. More often than not, this history was brutal under the Egyptians, the Assyrians, and perhaps to a lesser

---

[12] Müller, "Disciple, Follow, Imitate, After," 1:488.

degree, under the Babylonians. In the Greek OT (LXX) and in the NT, the primary word for this study is *doulos*, pronounced *doo'-los*. This word has also undergone some modifications in definition through the centuries and through the mingling of cultures.

In the secular Greek of the classical era, the doulos could not express his or her own will in word or in deed; the individual belonged, as property, to someone else. This is very similar to slavery experienced early in the history of the United States and Europe. Because people, by nature, cherish liberty, the doulos in any society is always looked down on. They might not always be treated poorly. In the classical Greek era, some had nearly the same status as free people, though this varied from one master to another. But the relationship of a doulos to master was always one that

> involved the abrogation of one's own autonomy and the subordination of one's will to that of another. ... on the whole, the life of the slave was one of unrelieved compulsory labour and service in the household and in public works.[13]

In ancient Greek culture, the citizen found his true worth in the full development of his own potential. The doulos was dependent and subordinate, hence usually despised.

In the OT, from the time of Abraham or Job through the

---

[13] R. Tuente, "Slave, Servant, Captive, Prisoner, Freedman," In *The New International Dictionary of New Testament Theology*, ed. Colin Brown (Grand Rapids: Zondervan, 1980), 3:593.

period of the kings, and depending on the culture, they could regard a servant as property, though the servant often possessed certain rights by law. A servant of Abraham, for example, was highly regarded, more akin to a vizier (Gn 24). But in the Greek OT, this is a different word, *pais,* which is related to doulos but not an exact synonym. According to the NIDNTT,

> The memory of Israel's experiences in their captivity in Egypt, "the house of slaves" (*bêt̲ 'ăb̲ād̲îm*; LXX *oikos douleias*, Exod. 13:3, 14) lingered on and was the main source of this root's essential meaning: it was distinguished from its synonyms (e.g. *diakoneō*) by its emphasis on the service being that of a slave, i.e. on a repressive or at least dependent form of service under the complete control of a superior.[14]

It is interesting, but not a discussion for this work, that the Bible does not outlaw slavery but regulates it in the law of Moses (Ex 21:1–11; Lv 25:39–55; Dt 15:1–18). The slave owner in Israel had different regulations for a slave of Hebrew extraction than for a slave taken from another nation, but the law prohibited the harsh conditions experienced by Israel under Egyptian bondage. Significantly, the law provided for someone to set the slave free after six years' service (Ex 21:1–11; Dt 15:12), and in the year of Jubilee (Lv 25:39–43, 47–55). Other ancient Near East legal codes, such as the Code of Hammurabi (ruler of Babylonia circa

---

[14] Tuente. "Slave, Servant, Captive, Prisoner, Freedman," 3:593.

2000 BC), were not as generous toward slaves as the law of God. Israel was unique.

In relation to God, Israel stood as servants (Jgs 2:7 [LXX], a cognate of doulos). They were aware, individually and corporately, of their position as servants of the Most High God (Ps 123:2), and "the Israelite was conscious of the infinite distance between him and his God and also of his complete dependence upon him."[15] They recognized God as Master and Judge but also as Savior in the Master/Judge/Savior relationship, while doulos "still retained the element of unconditional subjection to another, it yet lost the character of abject baseness."[16] The word *doulos*, through the special election of Israel and regarding Israel, took on a new dimension, one of honor as the chosen one. In this expanded definition, the community in relationship to God and humankind had an obligation to love and to serve one another (Lv 19:18). There was a certain dignity accorded to doulos as a servant of God and in serving each other. This was not the case in contemporary Greek culture.

With the mingling of the Greek and Jewish cultures because of the influence of Alexander the Great and the subsequent conquest of Israel by Rome, the word *doulos* assumes either a more Greek/Roman or Jewish interpretation depending on the context in which it is used. Hence, we must keep the foregoing discussion in mind as we look at the use of *doulos* in the NT. Perhaps the first thing we should note in the NT is that there are no objections raised to the distinction within the existing

---

[15] Tuente. "Slave, Servant, Captive, Prisoner, Freedman," 3:595.

[16] Tuente. "Slave, Servant, Captive, Prisoner, Freedman," 3:595.

social structure between slave and lord, bond and free. There is no condemnation of the practice of slavery, but neither is it promoted. Paul encouraged those bondservants who could to gain their freedom (1 Cor 7:21), and as in the law, the gospel compels masters to treat their slaves/servants as fellow heirs of the kingdom of God (Eph 6:9; Col 4:1). The NT assimilates both the Greek/Roman and the Jewish understandings of slavery or servanthood.

The NIDNTT states,

> In order to appreciate the nuances of meaning in the NT we must first see what its attitude is to the position of the slave in society. This can be found out principally from the parables of Jesus. Occasionally, slaves are put in a position of responsibility and command (Matt. 24:45). But the slave owes his master exclusive and absolute obedience (Matt. 8:9). "No one can serve as slave to two masters" (Matt. 6:24; Possessions, art. μαμωνᾶς). His work earned him neither profit nor thanks; he was only doing what he owed as a bondslave (Lk. 17:7–10). The master could use his unlimited power over his slave—for good (Matt. 18:27) or for unmerciful punishment if he were guilty of some fault (Matt. 18:34; 25:30).[17]

In the grand scheme of things, every person is subject to or a servant of God, either as a friend or as a foe. For those who

---

[17] Tuente, "Slave, Servant, Captive, Prisoner, Freedman," 3:595.

serve God through faith in Jesus Christ (Christians), some are put in positions of responsibility and command; each one owes his Master exclusive and absolute obedience; maybe his work will earn him neither profit nor thanks in this life. And the Master is sovereign with unlimited power over His slave, but He promises, "And we know that all things work together for good for those who love God, who are called according to his purpose" (Rom 8:28).

The best example of this in each instance is Jesus Christ Himself in relation to the Father:

> who, although He existed in the form of God, did not regard equality with God a thing to be grasped, but emptied Himself, taking the form of a bond-servant, and being made in the likeness of men. Being found in appearance as a man, He humbled Himself by becoming obedient to the point of death, even death on a cross. (Phil 2:6–8 NASB)

Jesus Christ exemplifies the servant of God perfectly.

What the Greeks and Romans did not know, and the Bible makes clear, is all people are born slaves to sin (Gn 6:5; Jer 17:9; Jn 8:34; Rom 6:16, 17), but the one who trusts in Christ, who the Son sets free, is free to serve Christ (Jn 8:35, 36). Given that in this life every person is the slave of either sin or of Christ, why not commit to being a slave of Christ? For this study, to be His slave you will owe Him your exclusive and absolute obedience. You cannot serve two masters, only Jesus. Your service earns you neither profit nor thanks in this life as you will only do what you owe as a bondslave. The Master can use His unlimited power over you. At times, it will appear to be good, at other times it may appear to be harsh, but His goodness, and His purpose to do good will be the rule.

Summary Definitions

Diligent

For this study, we understand *diligence* or *diligent* as "marked by careful and persistent work or effort."

Glory or Glorify

To do all to the glory of God is to honor Him and to enhance His reputation among humankind. When we leave a conversation or an event, we should have enhanced the reputation of God in the minds of those who have interacted with us.

Follow or Follower

As Jesus used the word, a follower, or to follow Jesus, means the person has found "a new settled purpose as He directs them into the true life."

Disciple

Following Jesus as a disciple means the unconditional sacrifice of one's whole life for the whole of one's life. To be a disciple means to be bound to Jesus and to do God's will.

Servant

To be His slave, you will owe Him your exclusive and absolute obedience; you cannot serve two masters, only Jesus. Your service may earn you neither profit nor thanks in this life as you will only do what you owe as a bondslave; the Master can use His unlimited power over you. At times it will appear to be good, at other times it may appear to be harsh, but His goodness and His purpose to do good will be the rule.

Study Questions

Regarding the doulos, or servant:
Why would I want to be His slave?

What level of humility would it require to live the life of a slave, bought and paid for?

Would it require any less or more humility to be a slave to the Lord Jesus, having been chosen, and bought and paid for?

What definitions did you not fully understand before? Is the correct definition hard for you to accept? How will your walk with Christ grow and change because of your new understanding?

The idea of being a servant is hard for some. Ask God to show you the true freedom of being His servant.

CHAPTER 2

THE NECESSITY OF DISCIPLESHIP

The church is facing a clear and present danger. It has in every generation. During my lifetime, the church in America has largely failed to make biblical disciples of the converts who have come into her. But the necessity of discipleship is as great today as it has ever been, as great as in the days of Jesus. Here we examine three reasons discipleship is necessary, even critical, in the church today.

First and foremost, it is necessary because Jesus commands it:

> Then Jesus came up and said to them, "All authority in heaven and on earth has been given to me. Therefore, go and make disciples of all nations, baptizing them in the name of the Father and the Son and the Holy Spirit, teaching them to obey everything I have commanded you. And

remember, I am with you always, to the end of the
age. (Mt 28:18–20)

In verse 19, Jesus said, "make disciples of all nations." The verb
"make disciples" is an imperative in the Greek; it's a command,
not a suggestion. Notice in verse 20, He says, "teaching them to
observe all that I have commanded you." In this diligence study,
we look at many of these commands in scripture. We need to learn
how to discern which of the scriptures are imperatives. It would
be easier if we could all read Greek and Hebrew, but few of us
can, so we depend on those who do to show us. Teaching people
to observe all that Jesus commanded might begin right here with
Matthew 28:19: make disciples—teach people how to live their
lives in ways to glorify God.

Second, there is a pressing need for discipleship because we
live in a world, in a nation, of biblically illiterate Christians. This
article is on the Fox News opinion page: "Why Are so Many
Christians Biblically Illiterate?"[1] In this article, author Dr.
Jeremiah J. Johnston states, "Most Christians know enough about
the Bible to be dangerous." Dr. R. C. Sproul authored a book
titled *Everyone's a Theologian*[2] in which he argues that everyone
has an opinion about God; the problem is not every opinion about
God is accurate. There is a certain hubris associated with quoting

---

[1] Jeremiah J. Johnston, "Why Are So Many Christians Biblically Illiterate?"
http://www.foxnews.com/opinion/2016/02/10/why-are-so-many-christians-
biblically-illiterate.html. Published February 10, 2016.

[2] R. C. Sproul, *Everyone's a Theologian: An Introduction to Systematic Theology*
(Sanford, FL: Reformation Trust Publishing, 2014).

the Bible, even when the quote is misleading and out of context. In Dr. Johnston's article, he writes,

> The Bible has become a moving target. One can strip it down, twist it, misread it, add to it, supplement it, and even overrule it, and, unfortunately, 95 percent of the congregation will not realize it.

Even among pastors in many of our mainstream denominations, the lack of biblical knowledge is appalling. The United Methodist Church has been in a fierce argument for years over homosexuality in the church, and more recently, in the pulpit. As I write this, the Methodist bishop for the region I live in is a practicing lesbian, whose base ignorance of the scriptures is embarrassing.

> As the UMC weighs the issue of whether to formally accept homosexuality, some in the denomination have already abandoned established church law. For example, Dr. Karen Oliveto is the first lesbian to be given the title of bishop in the UMC and has officiated at several same sex ceremonies at the UMC church she previously pastored. In August of last year, she wrote a sermon, also posted on Facebook, in which she calls Jesus a bigot and a changing, flawed human being.[3]

Here is a woman raised to a position of authority and leadership in the United Methodist Church, yet her life and her

---

[3] "UMC prolongs pro-gay push," *AFA Journal*, August 2018, p. 5.

teachings stand in stark disobedience to the book of discipline she has sworn to uphold.

Well-known researcher and evangelical Christian George Barna has written,

> The theological free-for-all that is encroaching in Protestant churches nationwide suggests the coming decade will be a time of unparalleled theological diversity and inconsistency.[4]

How else can you describe matters when most churchgoing adults reject the authority and the accuracy of scripture? We hear comments such as, "You don't really believe that story about the flood? And Jonah?" "Come on, a six-day creation, really?" Well, Jesus did. He talked about these events. Additional data show that most churchgoing adults reject the existence of Satan. They claim that Jesus sinned. They see no real need to evangelize because good works are one key to persuading God to forgive their sins. They also describe their commitment to Christianity as moderately or even less firm. Another study found that the most widely known Bible verse among adult and teen believers, people who say they are believers, is "God helps those who help themselves." That's not even in the Bible! When given thirteen basic teachings from the Bible, only 1 percent of adult believers firmly embrace all thirteen as biblical perspectives. The following statistic is from students at Wheaton College, a Bible college representing every state in the

---

[4] "Six Megathemes Emerge from Barna Group Research in 2010," https://www.barna.com/research/six-megathemes-emerge-from-barna-group-research-in-2010/ Published December 13, 2010.

nation and almost every Protestant denomination in the United States. NT professor Gary Burge revealed from questions he asked in his classes that one third of the students in Wheaton College could not put the following in the proper chronological order: Abraham, the OT prophets, the death of Christ, and Pentecost. That is tragic. As stated earlier, most Christians know just enough about the Bible to be dangerous. Most congregations across the nation don't realize when the Bible is being misused by their teacher/pastor, and they are being misinformed and misled.

The fault for widespread biblical illiteracy in the church lies within the church herself. In previous generations, children and young people were taught church doctrine using such works as *The Westminster Larger/Shorter Catechism* to have the requisite knowledge to read, understand, and argue works such as *The Westminster Confession of Faith*. Where pulpits had good expositional teaching of the scriptures, many pulpits today feature topical, or "hot-button" sermons, and parishioners remain ignorant of the overall context of any given passage of scripture. I am reminded of a quote, I know not its source: "Instead of feeding the sheep, they're entertaining the goats." Those who are ignorant of the scriptures cannot possibly make good progress in biblical discipleship.

By the time Jude wrote his letter to the saints, probably in the early to midsixties, there was already a body of doctrine that he could call "the faith that was once for all entrusted to the saints" (Jude 1:3). They developed this body of doctrine primarily from the OT and from discussions Jesus had with the disciples. The apostle Paul declared,

> Now I want you to know, brothers and sisters,
> that the gospel I preached is not of human origin.
> For I did not receive it or learn it from any human
> source; instead I received it by a revelation of Jesus
> Christ. (Gal 1:11–12)

Paul called this body of doctrine "the gospel of Christ" (Gal 1:7). This body of doctrine has not, will not, and cannot change. Because God is immutable, meaning He cannot change, then His Word does not, cannot change. What made up rebellion (and thus sin) against a holy God in the garden of Eden is still rebellion and sin against God in the garden of Gethsemane and in Central Park in New York City. The disciple of Christ must know the fundamentals of the faith.

The third reason for the necessity of discipleship is worldliness in the church. Paul wrote to Timothy,

> But understand this, that in the last days difficult
> times will come. For people will be lovers of
> themselves, lovers of money, boastful, arrogant,
> blasphemers, disobedient to parents, ungrateful,
> unholy, unloving, irreconcilable, slanderers,
> without self-control, savage, opposed to what
> is good, treacherous, reckless, conceited, loving
> pleasure rather than loving God. They will
> maintain the outward appearance of religion but
> will have repudiated its power. So avoid people
> like these. (2 Tm 3:1–5)

Jesus, in Matthew 24, spoke of false Christs, false prophets, and false teachers who would come in the last days. He said they would lead many astray, betraying one another, and hating one another. He urged us not to be alarmed, nor to be led astray. We are to persevere. We are in those days, and it will get worse before it gets better. Paul urged the church to be on guard:

> Be careful not to allow anyone to captivate you through an empty, deceitful philosophy that is according to human traditions and the elemental spirits of the world, and not according to Christ. (Col 2:8)

The line between biblical illiteracy and worldliness in the church is blurry. Those who don't know their Bibles are easy prey for the world. As mentioned previously, the United Methodist Church is weakening its stance on abortion; they come closer to the world every year. Now they are proposing a new position paper that would remove earlier cautionary statements and support abortion.[5]

Worldliness in the church is not a new problem; it is the reason that the glory of the Lord left the temple in Jerusalem. Ezekiel recorded the gripping account of this in Ezekiel chapters 8–11. In chapter 8, God shows the prophet, through visions, the abominations that occurred in the temple (vv. 3, 5, the image of

---

[5] Rev. Paul Stallworth, "United Methodist Church Proposes New Position Statement Saying "We Support Abortion"," https://www.lifenews.com/2018/08/28/united-methodist-church-proposes-new-position-statement-saying-we-support-abortion/.

jealousy), the abominations committed by the "house of Israel" (vv. 6, 9, 13), and "still greater abominations" (v. 15). It started with Solomon.

> When Solomon became old, his wives shifted his allegiance to other gods; he was not wholeheartedly devoted to the LORD his God, as his father David had been. Solomon worshiped the Sidonian goddess Astarte and the detestable Ammonite god Milcom. Solomon did evil in the LORD's sight; he did not remain loyal to the LORD, like his father David had. Furthermore, on the hill east of Jerusalem Solomon built a high place for the detestable Moabite god Chemosh and for the detestable Ammonite god Milcom. He built high places for all his foreign wives so they could burn incense and make sacrifices to their gods. (1 Kgs 11:4–8)

The situation finally degenerated to where God could not tell the difference between the "worship" services in the temples of the false gods across the valley and the "worship" services in the temple.

These abominations brought the wrath of God. In Ezekiel chapter 9, the wrath of God falls on Jerusalem. He sends six executioners to destroy the idolaters (9:1, 2). But first He sends a man clothed in linen with a writing case at his waist throughout the city to place a mark on the foreheads of all who groaned and mourned over all the abominations committed in the city (9:2–5,

11). In the ancient pictorial Hebrew, the 'mark' placed on the foreheads of those who would be spared was represented by two letters that looked like a cross and nail. In chapters 10 and 11, the glory of the Lord leaves the temple, and the wicked counselors are judged and condemned. When God can no longer discern the difference between our paganism and worship in the church, the time for judgment is ripe. We need to be about the business of purging the evil from the church instead of furthering the business of religion.

So the three points under the necessity of discipleship are because Jesus commands it, because the church is biblically illiterate, and because of worldliness in the church. It affects all of us. Everyone is a theologian. We have to be very careful who we listen to, what we read, and what videos we watch. We must be careful because with the increase in technology comes an increase in the influence of false teachers. They are out there, and they are ravenous toward the church.

Study Questions

Am I alarmed that Pew and Barna state that only 4 percent to 5 percent of Americans are true believers?

How much time and effort do I put into verifying the content of what is being taught in church / Sunday school / Bible study?

Take a moment (or a day) to pray about where your discipleship is in reality. Pray that God shows you where your theology is wrong. Journal your reflections. It will help keep you accountable throughout the rest of this study.

Take a good, honest look at your life. An inventory, if you will. Can God tell the difference between the way you live and the world? Write down your goals for how you would like to see your life and your worship of God be more like what He expects. Ask God to show you what this looks like. He will show you in His Word what your life should look like.

SECTION 2

THE PROCESS OF DISCIPLESHIP

CHAPTER 3

RENEWING THE MIND

As stated in the preface to this book, the goal of the Christian is to glorify God in our lives: nothing more, nothing less, nothing else. The scriptures support this. For example, "So whether you eat or drink, or whatever you do, do everything for the glory of God" (1 Cor 10:31); "And whatever you do in word or deed, do it all in the name of the Lord Jesus, giving thanks to God the Father through him" (Col 3:17). The Westminster Catechism supports this also, the first question of which is, "What is the chief and highest end of man?" The prescribed response is, "Man's chief and highest end is to glorify God, and fully to enjoy him forever." This is what we used to teach our children in earlier generations. The obvious problem in the effort to glorify God in all that we say and do is that "all have sinned and fall short of the glory of God" (Rom 3:23). While we "are justified by his grace as a gift, through the redemption that is in Christ Jesus, whom God put forward as a propitiation by his blood, to be received by faith" (Rom 3:24–25a ESV), it remains for us to make every effort to add to your faith excellence, to excellence, knowledge; to knowledge, self-control; to self-control, perseverance; to perseverance, godliness; to godliness, brotherly affection; to brotherly affection, unselfish love. For if these things are really yours and are continually increasing, they will keep you from becoming ineffective and unproductive in your pursuit of knowing our Lord Jesus Christ more intimately. (2 Pt 1:5–8)

We glorify God when we are fruitful: "My Father is honored by this, that you bear much fruit and show that you are my disciples" (Jn 15:8). Discipleship is behavior modification, the transformation of one's character.

To glorify God, we have to identify and eliminate events in our lives contrary to His holiness. I ask myself, "What does holiness look like in this event?" For example, a friend invited me to see a movie a few years ago. I had already looked it up on the internet site where I check movies because the story line was interesting to me. The review stated that there were over 150 f-words besides the names of God and Jesus being misused almost two dozen times; this in a movie that is approximately 120 minutes long. That is over one use of the f-word per minute. I asked my friend, "How is that holy?" If I go to the movie or rent the video, how do I explain to God that I paid people to curse Him and use that kind of language for my entertainment? We have to answer for that, you know.

Make a tree good and its fruit will be good, or make a tree bad and its fruit will be bad, for a tree is known by its fruit. Offspring of vipers! How are you able to say anything good, since you are evil? For the mouth speaks from what fills the heart. The good person brings good things out of his good treasury, and the evil person brings evil things out of his evil treasury. I tell you that on the day of judgment, people will give an account for every worthless word they speak. For by your words you will be justified, and by your words you will be condemned. (Mt 12:33–37)

My friend had already seen the movie and denied that the language was that bad. But he goes to movies much more frequently than I do, and he was so accustomed to that language he didn't even hear it anymore. That extreme language was not even offensive to him anymore. I do not want to get accustomed to that language. When we compromise the holiness of God, sin no longer offends us. We did not go to the movie, and since that incident, he now uses the same internet site to judge which movies are appropriate. He has reduced his movie time significantly. Develop the habit of asking yourself, "What does holy look like in this event?"

In this and the next several chapters, I define biblical discipleship and provide a five-step process to transform converts into maturing, fruit-bearing disciples of Jesus Christ. It is important to note that I could have built this model from any book of the Bible. The verses I chose represent the teaching of the whole Bible.

But first, a quick review is helpful. We have learned that to be a follower and a disciple of Jesus means we make a serious commitment, that we have found a new, settled purpose as God directs us into the true life. And it means the unconditional sacrifice of one's whole life for the whole of one's life. We are bound to Jesus to do His will. We have found that there is a pressing necessity for discipleship for three reasons: Jesus commanded it, because we live in a world and a culture of biblically illiterate Christians, and because of worldliness in the church.

Biblical discipleship is a process, ever-growing and never-ending. This is implied in 2 Peter 1:8.

> For if these things are really yours and are continually increasing, they will keep you from becoming ineffective and unproductive in your pursuit of knowing our Lord Jesus Christ more intimately.

Peter expects the disciple to continue in growth and to increase in fruitfulness. I have illustrated this with a diagram that looks like a staircase, but the fallacy of it is a sense of final accomplishment. There are only five steps; in the real world of discipleship, there is a beginning point but no end.

The five-step process is:

- Do not be conformed, but be transformed (Rom 12:1–2).
- Take every thought captive and make it obedient to Christ (2 Cor 10:5).
- Discipline your speech to benefit others (Eph 4:29).

- Glorify God in all that you say and do (1 Cor 10:31).
- Look like the biblical Jesus to the watching world (Phil 1:27).

As noted in the preface, in the parable of the sower, the crop with the highest yield came from the ground with the best prepared soil. In discipleship, the most fruitful among us is the person who has best prepared his or her mind as a fertile ground for the implanted seed. This is step 1, preparing the mind. Paul says this is a necessary first step before we can even know the will of God.

> I appeal to you therefore, brothers, by the mercies of God, to present your bodies as a living sacrifice, holy and acceptable to God, which is your spiritual worship. Do not be conformed to this world, but be transformed by the renewal of your mind, that by testing you may discern what is the will of God, what is good and acceptable and perfect. (Rom 12:1–2 ESV)

For our first step in this journey of discipleship, we dig into these two verses to better understand them.

In the statement "I appeal to you therefore," the Greek word translated "appeal" is *parakaleō*, pronounced *par-ak-al-eh'-o*. It's a compound word in the Greek, *para* meaning "the side of, alongside," and *kaleō* meaning "to call or summon." Paul, through a friendly exhortation, seeks to "come alongside" fellow believers and call them to action. He bases the call to action on "the mercies of God." What mercies? Paul has shown through compelling arguments that all Gentiles (non-Jews) are guilty of sin (Rom 1), and that all Jews are also guilty of sin (Rom 2). He concludes,

> What then? Are we better off? Certainly not, for we have already charged that Jews and Greeks alike are all under sin, just as it is written: "*There is no one righteous, not even one.* (Rom 3:9–10; emphasis added).

> for all have sinned and fall short of the glory of God. (Rom 3:23)

In chapters 3 through 7, he argues not only the improbability but the impossibility of meritorious salvation: "For *no one is declared righteous before him* by the works of the law, for through the law comes the knowledge of sin" (Rom 3:20; emphasis added). Having ruled out the possibility of works-based salvation, in these chapters he admits to the only other possibility, a faith-based salvation: "For what does the scripture say? 'Abraham believed God, and it was credited to him as righteousness'" (Rom 4:3), and "For the wages of sin is death, but the free gift of God is eternal life in Christ Jesus our Lord" (Rom 6:23 ESV).

Chapter 8 chronicles the great victory gained by the redeemed through Jesus Christ, beginning with "There is therefore now no condemnation for those who are in Christ Jesus" (Rom 8:1) and ending with,

No, in all these things we have complete victory through him who loved us! For I am convinced that neither death, nor life, nor angels, nor heavenly rulers, nor things that are present, nor things to come, nor powers, nor height, nor depth, nor anything else in creation will be able to separate us from the love of God in Christ Jesus our Lord. (Rom 8:37–39)

In chapters 9 through 11, using the only scriptures available to him, what we refer to as the OT, he writes about God's sovereign choice of certain Jews and Gentiles, who will become "the children of God" (Rom 9:8). These are the incredible "mercies of God" to which Paul makes mention.

Based on the incredible grace of the mercies of God, Paul encourages us to "present our bodies as a living sacrifice, holy and acceptable to God." In the sacrificial system, when a person brought a sacrifice to the priest, it was given lock, stock, and barrel. This was a free and voluntary offering. It was presented entirely, and the person released all claim or right to it. The priest was free to do all that the law required of him to that sacrificial offering, whether animal or grain, for the honor of God. The person who brought the sacrifice would not, could not take the offering back. Offering ourselves as a living sacrifice means that we give "our whole life, for the whole of our life" to God to do as He sees fit; no turning back. Paul urges believers to devote themselves entirely to God, to recognize no claim on themselves, to be disposed of by Him, to bear all that He might appoint, and to promote His honor (glory).

We are to be "holy and acceptable to God." About this (Rom 12:1), John Calvin comments,

> There are then two points to be considered here. First, we are the Lord's, and second, we ought for this very reason to be holy, for it is an affront to God's holiness, to offer him anything which has not first been consecrated. On this assumption it follows at the same time that we ought to meditate on holiness throughout the whole of our life, and that it is a kind of sacrilege if we relapse into uncleanness, for this is nothing but to profane what was sanctified.[1]

Some observe that the problem with a living sacrifice is that it wants to keep crawling off the altar. We must persevere; we must be diligent day by day, moment by moment to offer our lives to God for His purpose. We have no right to pursue our own interests apart from the counsel of God. Nor should we invent services which He does not appoint. The nineteenth-century pastor and biblical scholar Albert Barnes stated in his commentary on Romans 12:1,

---

[1] John Calvin, "Romans and Thessalonians," in *Calvin's New Testament Commentaries*, eds. David W. Torrance and Thomas F. Torrance, translated by Ross MacKenzie (Grand Rapids: Wm. B. Eerdmans, 1991), 263.

> They are to do just what God requires of them,
> and that will be acceptable to God. And this
> fact, that what we do is acceptable to God, is the
> highest recompense we can have. It matters little
> what men think of us, if God approves what we
> do. To please him should be our highest aim; the
> fact that we do please him is our highest reward.[2]

This sacrificial offering of ourselves, Paul says, is our spiritual service of worship. Considering the mercies of God shown to us, it is appropriate that we should give ourselves wholly to Him.

We could view Romans 12:1 as a general statement that the rest of chapters 12, 13, and 14 explain. Romans 12:1 is the "what," and 12:2–14:23 are the "how" of discipleship. In a further breakdown, Romans 12:2 is a general statement; we find the specifics in 12:3–14:23. Paul writes, "Do not be conformed to this world." We could read it as, "Do not be conformed any longer to the pattern of this world." We are born conformed to this world. In our flesh, we are born children of this world; we are products of this world. I love chocolate, and I am intrigued by the different forms carved into chocolate bars and candies. Most aren't hand carved. Chocolate is poured into a mold, cooked, and then released from the mold. We are born in the world's mold, but the world is against God.

> Do not love the world or the things in the world. If
> anyone loves the world, the love of the Father is not

---

[2] Albert Barnes, *Notes on the Bible,* http://onlinebible.net, 2012.

in him, because all that is in the world (the desire of
the flesh and the desire of the eyes and the arrogance
produced by material possessions) is not from the
Father, but is from the world. (1 Jn 2:15–16)

Biblical discipleship begins by breaking out of the mold of
the world. The problem is that the world has a strong hold on us,
similar to a strong rubber band, and we keep snapping back. We
must be diligent in being not conformed. It is in the imperative
in the Greek, a command, not a suggestion. We must identify
the patterns of the world, and then, through biblical arguments,
defeat them in our lives.

Be careful not to allow anyone to captivate you
through an empty, deceitful philosophy that is
according to human traditions and the elemental
spirits of the world, and not according to Christ.
(Col 2:8)

We are "transformed by the renewing" of our minds. The
verb translated "transformed" is in the imperative mood; it is a
command, not a suggestion. In putting off the rules, the morals of
men, we are to put on the rules, the morals of Christ. But not first
in the flesh for that is legalism. Paul bids us to be renewed in the
mind, which is the fountain of behavior. All behavior starts in the
mind and proceeds to our flesh. Our behavior reflects what our
minds dwell on, and our minds dwell on those things that capture
our passions. A true disciple is passionate for the things of Christ:
"If you love me, you will obey my commandments" (Jn 14:15). We

cannot put on the rules and morals of Christ if we are unfamiliar with them. Therefore, Jesus said to His disciples, "teaching them to obey everything I have commanded you."

We must take personal responsibility to learn the scriptures from qualified teachers. But the goal is not scripture memorization, nor to be the fastest to find a verse in the Bible. The goal is to know the scriptures well enough, to saturate the mind with the scriptures, so that our behavior in any and every event will align with the scriptures and promote the holiness of God.

Renewing the mind is the first of the five steps; it is foundational and cannot be short-circuited. Bible study is not optional; it is required and necessary. Whatever the competition for our time, Bible study has to be near the top of the list. It will probably be necessary to rearrange priorities and eliminate other activities to make adequate room. To be transformed, we have to extricate ourselves from the mold of the world by renewing our minds. That means being aware of everything that comes into our minds, We have to pay attention, and we have to make certain, as much as possible, to make that information part of being transformed. It means we don't watch certain movies, it means we don't watch certain TV shows, it means we don't listen to certain music, and we don't read certain books; we don't hang out in certain places or run with certain people because we must change our input, so we can get a different output. That's step 1.

Paul says,

> Let the word of Christ dwell in you richly,
> teaching and exhorting one another with all

wisdom, singing psalms, hymns, and spiritual
songs, all with grace in your hearts to God. And
whatever you do in word or deed, do it all in the
name of the Lord Jesus, giving thanks to God the
Father through him. (Col 3:16–17)

It is this renewing of the mind, letting the Word of Christ
dwell in us richly that will equip us to be transformed in our
behaviors. When we saturate our minds with the Word of God,
we are better equipped to test, approve, discern, and scrutinize
what is the good, acceptable, perfect will of God.

I earlier mentioned I could have built this model out of any, or
every book of the Bible. Peter also encourages us to be transformed
in our thinking and not conformed to the world.

Therefore, get your minds ready for action by
being fully sober, and set your hope completely
on the grace that will be brought to you when
Jesus Christ is revealed. Like obedient children,
do not comply with the evil urges you used to
follow in your ignorance, but, like the Holy One
who called you, become holy yourselves in all of
your conduct, for it is written, "You shall be holy,
because I am holy." (1 Pt 1:13–16)

Incidentally, in the scripture quoted above from Colossians
3:16, the word *let* is followed by the verb *dwell*. There really is not
a word in the Greek NT that directly translates "let"; the verb
demands it, and the verb is in the imperative mood, meaning that it

has the force of a command. This "letting the word of Christ dwell in you" is an activity under your control, and God commands you to do it. This refers back to the instructions of Christ: "teaching them to obey everything I have commanded you." We will see this again in step 3, so it is important to understand now, the force of a command, and the responsibility of *let*.

Study Questions

Paul rules out a meritorious salvation (cf. p. 36). Is there anything in me that is seeking salvation by my own effort?

In what areas do I compromise the holiness of God to satisfy myself?

After spending some time talking with God, list some ways that your life currently conforms to the pattern of the world.

What are some ways you will start to rearrange your priorities so that you will have more time to saturate your mind with the Word of God? Write these down so you can keep yourself accountable to working on change.

Write down the five-step process somewhere you will see it every day. Look up the verses in your Bible, and start meditating on them. Write the verse for step 1 on a three-by-five-inch card, and put it on your bathroom mirror or somewhere that you will see it throughout the day.

Examine me, O God, and probe my thoughts! Test me, and know my concerns! (Ps 139:23)

CHAPTER 4

Captivating the Mind

The second step in our diagram is to "take captive *every* thought to make it obedient to Christ" (2 Cor 10:5 NIV; emphasis mine). The NASB translation reads, "*We are* destroying speculations and every lofty thing raised up against the knowledge of God, and *we are* taking every thought captive to the obedience of Christ." Notice the words "we are" are in italics; they are supplied for clarity in our English translations. In the macrocontext of 1 and 2 Corinthians, Paul wrote to correct several practical and doctrinal issues that plagued the church. In this passage, Paul begins a defense of his ministry against some in the church who do not think he is a legitimate apostle. They doubt his ministry, thinking they are better equipped, better trained, and more spiritual. They accuse Paul and his helpers of "walking according to the flesh" (2 Cor 10:2 NASB). They have engaged Paul in warfare, a warfare of the minds. The method Paul uses to overcome this war is effective for us to use to overcome our "wars" with the world, the world we are not to conform to but to be transformed from.

How do we overcome the philosophy of a secular culture? A philosophy is a pattern of thinking that governs our lives. We all have a philosophy, whether or not we know it. Usually, this philosophy has to change. I refer again to Colossians 2:8 (ESV): "See to it that no one takes you captive by philosophy and empty deceit, according to human tradition, according to the elemental spirits of the world, and not according to Christ." Discipleship is behavior modification that leads to character transformation. This passage declares how we can overcome the pattern of thinking that governs our lives according to a secular culture. Do not be conformed but transformed. Some influential persons in the church in Corinth were stuck in their patterns of thinking, and they opposed Paul. There are some in our churches too and in our workplaces and communities. Once we understand the necessity of being transformed, step 2 is where we start.

The microcontext here is that we cannot solve the big picture without paying attention to the smaller picture. I can't put my world together unless I put myself together. If my world is in chaos, it's because my life is in chaos. Forget about the ills of the world that we think need to be corrected, which they surely do. If my life is in chaos, it's because I am in chaos. It starts right here. We're not talking about just the big things that we need to solve in our culture. We're talking about the little things that we need to solve in our personalities, in our characters, so we look like the biblical Jesus to a watching world. Remember this: thought gives rise to behavior. That's the microcontext, which I don't want us to miss. A person who does not govern every thought will never be fully transformed in the renewing of his or her mind. This hinders the discipleship progress.

There are three verbs in this verse that we need to pay particular attention to. All three are in the present tense, showing constant, ongoing activity. The first and third verbs are in the active voice, showing the author, Paul, is the one who initiates the action. The second verb is in the middle voice, showing that someone or something else initiates the action. All three verbs are participles, showing an *-ing* or *-ed* ending. The verbs are, in the NASB, "destroying," "raised," and "taking … captive." "Captive" is actually the verb, but it needs "taking" to make sense.

In order for Paul to be victorious in this warfare of the minds, he destroys speculations and arguments (present tense, active voice); speculations and arguments are raised against him (present tense, middle voice) by someone, or something else, for its own purpose. There is a purpose in the arguments raised against him. Who or what is raising the arguments is serving their own purpose(s). To be victorious, Paul has to take every thought captive (present tense, active voice), and he cannot let that thought escape his body unless he has made it obedient to the purpose(s) of Jesus Christ, his Master. And be sure Jesus Christ has a purpose for Paul in every situation. Think on this for just a moment. When we understand our callings as disciples and our positions in this world as servants of Jesus Christ, these verbs become more than words on a page. They become instructions for our warfare. It is my responsibility to recognize the world, the system of philosophy that opposes the rule of Christ in society and in me. It is my responsibility to engage such a philosophy in war, intending to destroy it in my life and in my segment of society. This is the transformation required in Romans 12:2 in step 1.

Imagine the transformative power released in our lives when we develop the discipline of taking every thought captive and then not allowing it to escape unless we have made it obedient to the purpose of Christ. And the purpose of Christ is to bring glory to the Father, to enhance His reputation. That means we have to fashion all our words, all our body language, and all our tone of voice to bring glory to God. Therefore, we must ask ourselves, "What does holiness look like in this situation, in this event?"

Think back on the life of Christ in the Gospels. When did He fail to glorify God in His response, in His conversation, or in His tone of voice? He never did. In the same way, we can train ourselves to glorify God. Peter wrote in his second letter that God has already given us everything we need for life and godliness through our knowledge of God, who called us by His own glory and goodness (2 Pt 1:3). According to Peter, when we come to the cross, confess our sins, and ask Jesus for forgiveness, at that instant, God gives us all the tools we need for life and godliness. It is then our responsibility to learn how to use the tools. This is the process of discipleship, learning how to glorify God in all that we say and do.

It is our responsibility, as disciples of Christ, to bear much fruit (Jn 15:8). The fruit God is looking for is a transformed character.

> For this is God's will: that you become holy. (1 Thes 4:3)

For God wants you to silence the ignorance of foolish people by doing good. (1 Pt 2:15).

So, since Christ suffered in the flesh, you also arm yourselves with the same attitude, because the one who has suffered in the flesh has finished with sin, in that he spends the rest of his time on earth concerned about the will of God and not human desires (1 Pt 4:1–2)

Good works, or works of righteousness, will proceed from a transformed character (Eph 2:10). Notice in 2 Peter 1:3 we are "called." Peter writes that God has already given us everything we need for life and godliness. God enables those He calls, but the development of a godly character is not automatic. Peter urges us in verse 5 "to make every effort" or to "apply all diligence" in the formation of a godly character.

What exactly does Peter intend when he urges us to apply all diligence or to make every effort? I try to make my efforts in discipleship match the efforts of an Olympic contender and champion. The first consideration is what priority I should give this. No price is too high when we consider the return on investment. A proper emphasis on discipleship will render most self-help books irrelevant. It is very hard to take every thought captive and make it obedient to the purpose of Christ. But as with any discipline, it gets easier the more we work at and think about it. To the extent we learn to take our thoughts captive and make them obedient to the purpose of Christ *before* we let them escape from our bodies, we will experience a corresponding benefit in our relationships. A proper understanding of the relationship of a disciple and servant dictates that our first—and highest—priority is to serve the Master and to learn of Him. To be like Him is our highest priority. Dr. R. C. Sproul, in *The Reformation Study Bible*, states in the notes on 2 Corinthians 10:5, "If every thought, then the whole person—every idea, motive, desire, and decision—belongs to Christ."[1] As servants of God, He owns us: "every idea, motive, desire, and decision—belongs to Christ." This is what Paul intends for us to grasp.

From Dr. Sproul we move to one of my favorites from the late 1800s, Albert Barnes. He comments on this verse: "the various systems of false philosophy were so entrenched that they might be called the stronghold of the enemies of God."[2] Let me ask you a question pertaining to this comment. Is there some pattern of your thinking governing your life, your philosophy, that is entrenched in your character but is actually a stronghold of the enemy of God? A prime example is sarcasm. I have found that sarcasm, ninety-nine times out of a hundred, is sin and a stronghold of the enemy of God. There is so little beneficial sarcasm that the best policy is to abstain completely, and you can't do that unless you're willing to take every thought captive. Sarcasm in a person's life becomes an enemy of God, a stronghold. Instead of "stronghold" in 2 Corinthians 10:4, the NASB translates it "fortress." Here is how to tear down strongholds: take every thought captive and make it obedient to Christ. And we can do that because God has already given us everything we need for life and godliness. He

---

[1] Excerpt From: R.C. Sproul. *The Reformation Study Bible.* iBooks.

[2] Albert Barnes, *Notes on the Bible,* http://onlinebible.net, 2012.

has given us the power to control our languages, our thoughts, and our behaviors.

Dr. Barnes makes another comment here: "all of the emotions and feelings of the heart should be controlled by Him, and led by Him, as a captive is led by a victor."[3] Take every thought captive and make it obedient to Christ. The word-picture in the Greek is literally of a fortress where the enemy lives—perhaps that is your heart—and the troops of God, led by Jesus Christ, are coming against that fortress. They blow the trumpet and tear down the walls of that fortress and of your heart, and Christ, the King of Kings, comes marching in. There is a great battle being fought, a war waged within the confines of that fortress. Who will win? This is where we come to that intersection between the sovereignty of God and our responsibility. Who will win that battle for the fortress of your heart? You can if you want. Or you can stand against God and grieve the Holy Spirit of God, who sealed you for the day of redemption (Eph 4:30).

It is possible to resist the Holy Spirit when He comes to convict you of sin and of judgment and of righteousness as in John 16:8–11. You can refuse His discipline, and far too many in the church are doing just that. Listen to them: "Okay, okay, I'll go to church. I'll put a dollar in the offering. I'll watch my language while I'm there." That is not what God wants. That is not victory; that's defeat. That heart is a stronghold for the enemies of God. What God wants is no less than your best; always. Dr. Barnes says that God should control all the emotions and feelings of the heart. So we let Him in, and He cleanses our hearts. We get a

---

[3] Barnes, *Notes on the Bible,* http://onlinebible.net, 2012.

grip on that sarcasm, we get a grip on that foul language, we get a grip on those thoughts that take us away from the holiness of God, and we give them to Jesus, making them obedient to Christ.

Recap: The responsibility of every disciple of Christ is to make certain that his or her life, at all times and in all ways, glorifies God as stated in the Westminster Larger Catechism. First, we need to understand that we have a responsibility before God not to be conformed to the pattern of this world; the renewing of our minds should transform us. Then the next step is the renewing of our minds by taking control of our thoughts and not letting a single thought escape our bodies until we have made it obedient to Jesus Christ. It is our tone of voice, it is the gestures we use, it is our choice of words, it is the goal of our conversation. The goal of our conversation comes in the next step.

Study Questions

Write step two on a three-by-five-inch card, and place it next to the card for step 1. Ask God for the conviction of the Holy Spirit in taking every thought captive.

What can I do, big or small, to help promote victory for myself in this "warfare of the mind"?

Is there anything I need to confess, anyone I need to apologize to for habitually using harsh words or a harsh tone?

Is there someone I could bring in to help hold me accountable in this endeavor of character transformation, someone who will encourage and not beat me up with it?

What is there in my life that impedes my ability to take control of my thoughts? Examples in this chapter were sarcasm or foul language. Is yours rolling your eyes or disrespectful speech? Write about it, and then write specific goals for how you will change this by taking your thoughts captive before they become actions.

CHAPTER 5

EXPRESSING THE MIND

In step 1 of the process of discipleship, we considered Romans 12:1–2. We are duty bound to offer ourselves, our bodies, to God as living sacrifices. He *commands us* to recognize the strategies of the world, to extract ourselves from them, and to be transformed by the renewing of our minds. We memorize and meditate on the Word to move it into our hearts, to weave it into the fabric of our lives so it becomes a part of our being. In step 2 we learned that Paul overcame the philosophies of the world and false philosophies in the church, breaking down strongholds by recognizing the strategies of the world, taking his thoughts captive, and planning well-devised defenses before he responded. He did not allow his thoughts to escape his body unless he made them captive to the purpose(s) of Christ. We learned that thoughts govern the words we use, the tone of voice that we use, and the expressions we make with our faces and our eyes. Thoughts govern all our behaviors.

In step 3 we consider how to express our thoughts once we

have taken them captive and made them obedient to the purpose of Christ. For this step we will examine Ephesians 4:29–32 (NIV):

> Do not let any unwholesome talk come out of your mouths, but only what is helpful for building others up according to their needs, that it may benefit those who listen. And do not grieve the Holy Spirit of God, with whom you were sealed for the day of redemption. Get rid of all bitterness, rage and anger, brawling and slander, along with every form of malice. Be kind and compassionate to one another, forgiving each other, just as in Christ God forgave you.

These verses teach us a lot about how to govern our behaviors. Remember, discipleship is behavior modification, the transformation of one's character.

In verse 29, there are two verbs translated in the NIV as "come out" and "listen." The first, "come out," is an imperative; it is a command. It is in the present tense, showing constant vigilance. The second, "listen," is a present tense, active voice participle; someone is always listening to the words we speak.

The command "come out" is a negative command, thus the NIV translates "do not let." Again, there is no word in the Greek text for *let*, but we need it for our English translations. When *let* is used with a verb in the imperative, followed by the third person, as this is, "it implies permission or command to an inferior."[1] It shows that whatever is being commanded, either permitted or prohibited, is under the absolute control of the person.

Here the definition of a servant is important. We owe Him our exclusive and absolute obedience. He is the Sovereign King of the universe; we do not have the right to question or excuse His commands. He commands, "Do not let." Paul, writing under the inspiration of the Holy Spirit and with the authority of Jesus Christ, addresses us as inferiors—not to him, to Jesus—with this command, "Do not let."

One might wonder what "unwholesome talk" is. Unwholesome talk is defined by the opposite in the same verse: "but only what is helpful for building others up according to their needs." Building others up according to their needs is contextually defined as wholesome talk. Therefore, any talk that does not build others up *according to their needs* is, by definition, unwholesome.

I stated in step 2 that sarcasm is almost always a sin. Stop to consider this for a moment. As disciples of Christ, servants of the Most High God, He does not permit us to say anything to anyone except that we design it to build them up according to their needs. To edify is the act of one who promotes another's growth in Christian wisdom, piety, happiness, and holiness. When we take this command seriously, as we have to if we are disciples of Christ, this means a lot of "shut up" time. The point of taking our thoughts captive is to restrict them from leaving our bodies until we make them captive to the purpose of Christ. Paul states that

---

[1] Noah Webster, *Webster's 1828 Dictionary of American English,* Public Domain, 1828.

the purpose of our conversation is always to encourage and edify the person to whom we speak. My father used to tell me, "If you have nothing good to say, don't say it here." Jesus says, "I do not permit you to say anything except that it builds up or edifies the person to whom you are speaking."

There are two more conditions. Our words must edify people according to their needs. According to *The Expositor's Greek Testament,* this statement means "edification applied to the need."[2] This means we have to listen to them and know them or their situations well enough to speak intelligently and to target their needs. There just is not room for careless conversation.

The final condition is that our words must also take into consideration anyone who may listen "that it may benefit" or "give grace" to those who listen. The thing with servants and disciples is they are never off the clock. Jesus warned the Pharisees,

> But I tell you that everyone will have to give account on the day of judgment for every empty word they have spoken. For by your words you will be acquitted, and by your words you will be condemned. (Mt 12:36–37 NIV)

In the preface, I stated that I hold firmly to salvation by grace through faith. I am not proposing a loss of salvation by careless words, but the scriptures never encourage "empty words." Oh, be careful, little mouth, what you say. Rather,

---

[2] S.D.F. Salmond, "Ephesians," in *The Expositor's Greek Testament,* ed. W. Robertson Nicholl, (New York: George H. Doran Co., public domain), vol. 3, loc. cit.

Let the word of Christ dwell in you richly, teaching and admonishing one another in all wisdom, singing psalms and hymns and spiritual songs, with thankfulness in your hearts to God. (Col 3:16 ESV)

Let the words of my mouth and the meditation of my heart be acceptable in Your sight, O LORD, my rock and my Redeemer. (Ps 19:14 NASB)

My mouth shall speak wisdom; the meditation of my heart shall be understanding. (Ps 49:3 ESV)

Here is the bottom line: If we are not constantly planning our speech on all occasions, we will end up using empty, careless, evil words, words that you might not want to give an account for. The Holy Spirit will help us build wholesome speech, but we are also to take personal responsibility for our speech.

Verse 30 says, "And do not grieve the Holy Spirit of God, by whom you were sealed for the day of redemption." This verse has two verbs, *grieve* and *sealed*. *Grieve* is used in the present tense, active voice, and it is an imperative, a command. The present tense shows a continuous activity, and the active voice shows that the person involved starts the activity; the grievous activity is under the complete control of the person. This again is a negative command, "Do not grieve." Sandwiched between verses 29 and 31, it shows that the activities in those verses do, in fact, grieve or distress the Holy Spirit. When we are not careful with our words, or if we give haven to bitterness, wrath, anger, clamor, slander, and malice, we actively work against the Holy Spirit of God. This is sin.

Corrupt thoughts come and go through our minds; it is impossible to prevent them. If we do not take control of them, they will not only leave trails, they will leave puddles of pollution. We must learn to take our thoughts captive and make them obedient to the purpose of Christ. If we do not, we will have trails and puddles of pollution that will give birth to behavior that grieves the Holy Spirit.

It is this Holy Spirit by whom we have been "sealed" for the day of redemption, the second verb in this verse. This verb is different. It is used in the aorist tense, a particular point in time. The passive voice shows the action is done to the recipient by another, not by the recipient; and the indicative mood indicates it is a statement of fact. The Christian is sealed one time and not of his or her own doing. It is a done deal, an accomplished fact. Since this is the case, we are duty bound to live accordingly. Jesus said, "teaching them to obey everything I have commanded you" (Mt 28:20). If we continue to grieve the Holy Spirit, the question must be asked, "Am I really a child of God?" Charles Spurgeon, arguably the most widely read preacher in history, has said,

> "You are to give Him the name Jesus, because *He will save His people from their sins.*" (Matthew 1:21) Many people think that, when we preach salvation, we mean salvation from going to Hell. We do mean that, but we mean a great deal more. We preach *salvation from sin.* We say that Christ

is able to save a man; and we mean by that, that He is able to save him from sin and to make him holy—to make him into a new man. No person has any right to say, "I am saved," while he continues in sin as he did before. *How can you be saved from sin, while you are living in it?* You will always know whether you are delivered from the guilt and condemnation of sin, by answering this question: *"Am I delivered from the love of sin?"* It is faith that saves us—not works. But that faith which saves us, always produces works. Does the world satisfy you? Then you have your reward and portion in this life. Make much of it—for you shall know no other joy! If your religion does not make you holy—it will damn you! It is simply painted pageantry to go to Hell in! If you have *lived* like the wicked—then you will *die* like the wicked, and be *damned* like the wicked![3]

Sin grieves the Holy Spirit of God, and God does not compromise sin; He does not suffer fools. Romans chapter 7 illustrates, in the opinion of many scholars, the lifelong struggle against sin. We cannot live a life of sinless perfection, but Peter insists that the qualities of Christian character, piety, should increase in our lives over time (2 Pt 1:8). If you want to be known

---

[3] Cited from *Grace Gems!* http:\\www.gracegems.org, Today's Grace Gem, 9/25/2018.

as a disciple of Jesus Christ, it is your personal responsibility to stand up and do it every day, all the time, until you die.

Verse 31 says, "Let all bitterness and wrath and anger and clamor and slander be put away from you, along with all malice" (ESV). Here again, we have the word *let*, and it means the same here as in verse 29. It shows that whatever is being commanded, either permitted or prohibited, is under the absolute control of the person.

The NIV translates the beginning of the verse as "Get rid of all." The verb in this verse is, in the ESV, "be put away"; in the NIV, it is, "Get rid of." Grammatically, the ESV is probably closer, as the verb is in the aorist tense, a particular point in time. It is in the passive voice, indicting action done to the recipient, but it is an imperative, a command. This is an action started by the Holy Spirit, but the individual must participate in his or her rescue; you must work with the Holy Spirit. We are not talking about anger management; we are talking about getting rid of anger, or as I call it, anger-get-rid-of-it-ment. We don't want to manage our anger; we want to get rid of it, along with any malice (ill-will toward others) and the other harsh behaviors listed in this verse. They are contrary to piety, to holiness.

Francis Foulkes, writing in the *Tyndale New Testament Commentary* series, remarks on this verse regarding the word *malice*: "Lastly the apostle adds *all malice*, 'bad feeling of every kind' (NEB), thus demanding the complete exclusion from the Christian's life of every thought that leads a person to speak or do evil against another."⁴ The only way we can do this is to return to step 2: take every thought captive to make it obedient to the purpose of Christ.

When we discipline ourselves to know the patterns of the world, to be transformed by the renewing of our minds, to take every thought captive to the purpose of Christ, then these bad behaviors listed here will not dominate our lives. We will recognize them, arrest them, and finally reject them. But reject them in favor of what? Remember to ask yourself, "What does holiness look like in this situation, this event?" Holiness looks like verse 32.

Verse 32 says, "Instead, be kind to one another, compassionate, forgiving one another, just as God in Christ also forgave you." Read that again. Those words just taste good rolling off the tongue. Wouldn't you prefer if those in your social circle strived to treat you with the considerations of this verse, instead of those in the previous verse? I would. Why don't we do that? Because we are born conformed to the image of this world and not instructed very well in the diligence of discipleship. It is hard work to do well, to act well, to *be* good. That is why Peter wrote to us, "applying all diligence." He knew how hard it is to just do this verse. But hard is not impossible; it is a matter of choice.

There are three verbs in this verse. "Be," or "cause to be," used in the present tense shows constant activity, and it is an imperative, a command—be kind! The verb "to be" is constructed in the

---

⁴ Francis Foulkes, "The Epistle of Paul to the Ephesians: An Introduction and Commentary." in *Tyndale New Testament Commentaries: A Concise, Workable Tool for Laymen, Teachers and Ministers,* edited by R. V. G. Tasker. (Grand Rapids, MI: Wm. B. Eerdmans 1956, Reprinted 1981), 137.

middle voice, which means you are to be kind, tenderhearted, and forgiving because of who you are, and in accord with your purpose. Your kindness, tenderheartedness, and forgiveness are not conditioned on, or by, the other person; it reflects who you are or should be. Be tenderhearted! The other verbs are "forgiving" and "forgave." "Forgiving" is associated with "be," and it is a participle—be forgiving! The third verb, "forgave," is associated with God, is in aorist tense, and is an indicative—a statement of fact. In fact, God has forgiven you, therefore, forgive each other.

The kind person is obliging, benevolent, mild, and pleasant (opposed to harsh, hard, sharp, and bitter). Forgiveness is a fruit of kindness. The tenderhearted person is compassionate, which is:

> Having a temper or disposition to pity; inclined to show mercy; merciful; having a heart that is tender, and easily moved by the distresses, sufferings, wants and infirmities of others.[5]

To forgive is to grant a pardon *and to treat the person as not guilty,* as if the offense had not occurred. This is how God forgives us, and we are to forgive as God has forgiven us (in the same manner, Mt 6:12). Francis Foulkes summarizes this verse and these several verses in this statement: "The eradication of evil words and actions depends ultimately on the purification of the thought life."[6] Exactly. Purification of the thought life is necessary, but purification is not complete until we remove the

[5] Webster, "*Webster's 1828 Dictionary of American English.*"
[6] Foulkes, "The Epistle of Paul to the Ephesians: An Introduction and Commentary."

pollution. We must identify what being conformed to this world looks like and then transform and renew our minds. We must discipline ourselves to take every thought captive and not let it escape our bodies until it is obedient to the purpose of Christ. We must plan our speech so every word edifies others. We must abandon all harsh, unholy behaviors that grieve the Holy Spirit and replace them with behaviors that glorify God. But what does it mean to "glorify God"? This is the next step—step 4.

Study Questions

Who is the most aggravating person in my world? How can I purify my thoughts regarding that person? Does God love that person?

Can I imagine that person stamped with the words, "Handle with Care"? Am I able to show compassion, be tenderhearted, and thereby pleasing to God in my care for this person? (Try it, and feel God smile.)

What are some examples of "unwholesome talk" that you could cut out of your speech?

What does it mean to you to forgive? Do you have a biblical view of forgiveness?

When you think of a kind person, what comes to mind? Do you fit this description?

CHAPTER 6

To God Be the Glory

In diagram 1, step 4 states, "Everything we do, small or great, should glorify God." I base this on 1 Corinthians 10:31 (NASB): "Whether, then, you eat or drink or whatever you do, do all to the glory of God." We are reminded of the Westminster Catechism, of which the first question is, "What is the chief and highest end of man?" And the response is, "Man's chief and highest end is to glorify God, and fully to enjoy Him forever." To glorify God is the object of step 4 in *The Diligence of Discipleship*.

In chapter 1, "Definitions," we learned that to do all to the glory of God is to honor Him and to enhance His reputation among humankind. When we leave a conversation or an event, we should enhance the reputation of God in the minds of those with whom we have interacted. I stated in the preface that the goal of Christian life is to glorify God, nothing more, nothing less, nothing else. I also stated that this process of discipleship would be the hardest exercise you have ever undertaken because it requires the complete transformation of who you are, but it would also be the most rewarding to improving your relationships with others. This is because when we glorify God, we recede. As John the Baptizer stated, "He must increase, but I must decrease" (Jn 3:30 ESV), or in the NET, "He must become more important while I become less important." It is our task to turn people toward Jesus and divert attention away from ourselves. When we focus our attention on ourselves, we are seeking our own glory to gratify ourselves. To glorify God, we must,

> Do nothing from selfish ambition or conceit, but in humility count others more significant than yourselves. Let each of you look not only to his own interests, but also to the interests of others. (Phil 2:3–4 ESV)

To set this verse in context (1 Cor 10:31), Paul addresses several problems in the church in Corinth. He learned of these conflicts in a letter from them. In chapter 8, Paul begins a discussion regarding food offered to idols and whether the believer should eat this food. Essentially, his argument on this revolves around self-denial; the brother or sister who has a clear conscience regarding this should not eat if there is the possibility of offending another brother. He illustrates this same argument in chapter 9, where he argues from his own practice of self-denial regarding not taking support from some churches for his ministry, which he was entitled to. In chapter 10, he warns against relapsing into idolatry, as did the children of Israel coming out of Egypt.

The eating of food sacrificed to idols is not as big a problem as is the danger of idolatry when we are not careful of our associations.

We associate with other Christians in partaking of the Lord's table, but there is a participation with idolaters when we partake with them (10:6–13). Finally, Paul states that

> "Everything is lawful," but not everything is beneficial. "Everything is lawful," but not everything builds others up. Do not seek your own good, but the good of the other person. (1 Cor 10:23–24)

We are to seek the good of our neighbor, not our own. And in this we glorify God. Paul's conclusion is,

> So whether you eat or drink, or whatever you do, do everything for the glory of God. Do not give offense to Jews or Greeks or to the church of God, just as I also try to please everyone in all things. I do not seek my own benefit, but the benefit of many, so that they may be saved. Be imitators of me, just as I also am of Christ. (1 Cor 10:31–11:1)

The verb Paul uses in verse 31, "do," is in the present tense, active voice, and is an imperative, a command. Thus, he commands us to always (present tense) take the responsibility on ourselves (active voice) to glorify God, to enhance His reputation in whatsoever we do, even in such mundane things as eating and drinking. This is the imitation of Christ (11:1). When the apostle adds the phrase "or whatever you do," he removes this command from the strict contextual observance of food sacrificed

73

to idols. He makes this a general direction for all of life, whatever situation we find ourselves in. We learn to ask ourselves, "What does holiness look like in this situation?"

Albert Barnes, in his commentary on this verse stated, "Or whatsoever ye do—In all the actions and plans of life; whatever be your schemes, your desires, your doings, let all be done to the glory of God."[1] Schemes, desires, and doings. We plan these events. The Christian who lives to glorify God lives intentionally, with a purpose. Because of our corrupted human nature, if we do not plan to glorify God, then we will not. If we do not glorify God, we will disgrace Him. We should not, and cannot, depend on accidents to glorify God. There must be an efficient, intelligent cause with design. Some say, "If you fail to plan, you plan to fail."

Dr. Lange states in his *Commentary on the Holy Scriptures*, "Our conduct can not glorify unless it be our object to act for His glory."[2] It must be our purpose, our design, to act for His glory in everything we do. Dr. Lange further states, quoting Dr. Hodge,

> Let self be forgotten. Let your eye be fixed on God. Let the promotion of His glory be your object in all ye do. Strive in every thing to act in such a way that men may praise that God whom you profess to serve.[3]

---

[1] Albert Barnes, *Notes on the Bible,* http://onlinebible.net, 2012.

[2] Christian Friedrich Kling, "The First Epistle of Paul to the Corinthians," in Lange's *Commentary on the Holy Scriptures*, ed. John P. Lange, (BibleWorks electronic edition, 2017).

[3] Lange, *Commentary on the Holy Scriptures.*

In the first step of this process, I mentioned that I could have built this model from any book of the Bible, and the verses I chose represent the teaching of the whole Bible. Let's consider some other verses that show the truth of glorifying God in all that we do.

> Just as each one has received a gift, use it to serve one another as good stewards of the varied grace of God. Whoever speaks, let it be with God's words. Whoever serves, do so with the strength that God supplies, *so that in everything God will be glorified through Jesus Christ.* To him belong the glory and the power forever and ever. Amen. (1 Pt 4:10–11; emphasis added)

We glorify God by using our spiritual gifts to serve one another. Paul states the same principle in Philippians:

> Do nothing from selfish ambition or conceit, but in humility count others more significant than yourselves. Let each of you look not only to his own interests, but also to the interests of others. (Phil 2:3–4 ESV)

And in Colossians,

> Let the word of Christ dwell in you richly, teaching and exhorting one another with all wisdom, singing psalms, hymns, and spiritual

songs, all with grace in your hearts to God. And whatever you do in word or deed, do it all in the name of the Lord Jesus, giving thanks to God the Father through him. (Col 3:16–17)

The whole of scripture, beginning to end, requires that the faithful live for the glory of God, not their own.

The title of this book is taken from 2 Peter 1:5 (NASB): "Now for this very reason also, applying all diligence." Peter begins this epistle urging diligence, and he ends it with the same urgency. In his closing exhortation (2 Pt 3:11–18), he urges the life of "holiness and godliness" (v. 11). "We are waiting for new heavens and a new earth, in which righteousness truly resides" (v. 13). Since then we are waiting. It behooves to practice that life of righteousness now. We will finally trade our history of sin for a new life of absolute purity. Imagine a world where every aspect, every being is as holy as God is. Let's practice now!

In verse 14 (ESV), he urges the believer to "be diligent to be found in him without spot or blemish, and at peace." Peter closes his letter with the statement, concerning Jesus Christ, "To him be the honor both now and on that eternal day." The word *honor* here is the same Greek word we have looked at elsewhere translated "glory." It is our duty, our responsibility, our goal to bring glory to our Savior, Jesus Christ. Once alerted to this principle of glorifying God in all we do, you will no doubt find this on nearly every page in your Bible.

Here are more good commentaries on 1 Corinthians 10:31. From Albert Barnes:

Do all to the glory of God—The phrase "the glory of God" is equivalent to the honor of God; and the direction is, that we should so act in all things as to "honor" him as our Lawgiver, our Creator, our Redeemer; and so as to lead others by our example to praise him and to embrace His gospel … This rule is designed to be one of the chief directors of our lives. It is to guide all our conduct, and to constitute a "test" by which to try our actions. Whatever can be done to advance the honor of God is right; whatever cannot be done with that end is wrong. Whatever plan a man can form that will have this end is a good plan; whatever cannot be made to have this tendency, and that cannot be commended, continued, and ended with a distinct and definite desire to promote His honor, is wrong, and should be immediately abandoned … What a change would it make in the world if this rule were everywhere followed! How differently would even professing Christians live! How many of their plans would they be constrained at once to abandon! And what a mighty revolution would it at once make on earth should all the actions of people begin to be performed to promote the glory of God![4]

---

[4] Barnes, *Notes on the Bible,* http://onlinebible.net, 2012

From John Calvin:

> Paul teaches that there is no part of our life or conduct, however insignificant, which should not be related to the glory of God, and that we must be concerned, in eating and drinking, to do all we can to promote it.[5]

John Gill, in his commentary on this verse, writes,

> the glory of God should be the end of all our actions: besides, without this no action can be truly called a good one; if a man seeks himself, his own glory, and popular applause, or has any sinister and selfish end in view in what he does, it cannot be said, nor will it be accounted by God to be a good action.[6]

Matthew Henry writes,

> The apostle takes occasion from this discourse to lay down a rule for Christians' conduct, and apply it to this particular case (1 Co 10:31, 32), namely, that in eating and drinking, and in all we do, we

---

[5] John Calvin, "The First Epistle of Paul the Apostle to the Corinthians," in *Calvin's New Testament Commentaries,* eds. David W. Torrance and Thomas F. Torrance, trans. by John W. Fraser, (Grand Rapids: Wm. B. Eerdmans, 1989), 224.

[6] John Gill, *The New Exposition of the Bible,* (Winterborne, Canada: Larry Pierce, 2002).

should aim at the glory of God, at pleasing and honouring him. This is the fundamental principle of practical godliness. The great end of all practical religion must direct us where particular and express rules are wanting. Nothing must be done against the glory of God, and the good of our neighbours, connected with it ... Our own humour and appetite must not determine our practice, but the honour of God and the good and edification of the church. We should not so much consult our own pleasure and interest as the advancement of the kingdom of God among men. Note, A Christian should be a man devoted to God, and of a public spirit.[7]

In our natural state, we conform to the world; we are self-centered. Transformation requires constant effort on our part (Rom 12:2). In our natural state, we seek our own glory, not the glory of others and not the glory of God. A necessary part of the transformation Paul commands in Romans 12:2 is to learn by the renewing of our minds to seek the glory of God in all that we do. This is not like learning math formulas, where once learned, we always apply them as the default. Once we memorize the multiplication tables, we can instantly recall them. This is not how it works with learning to glorify God. Every event is a new situation and demands a fresh response to our question,

---

[7] Matthew Henry, *Revised Matthew Henry Commentary.* (Winterbourne, Ontario. Timnathserah Inc. 1997).

"What does holiness look like in this situation?" Will my response honor God, and how will I enhance His reputation? True biblical discipleship requires this attention to detail in every waking minute. All events, no matter how mundane, are sacred when lived in the presence of God (*Coram Deo*).

In the presence of God. I had a youth pastor who used an illustration, and it has stuck with me. Suppose you get your white shirt dirty, so you launder it. When seen under a 40-watt light bulb, it looks clean. But in a different room, under a 60-watt bulb, stains appear that you didn't see in the lesser light. So you wash it again, with bleach. Now it looks good even under the 60-watt bulb. But in the daylight, under the bright sun, there are more stains visible! Wash it again! And so it goes. The greater the intensity of the light, the more obvious are the imperfections. The closer we draw to Jesus Christ, the Light of the World, the better able we are to see the corruption in ourselves and in the world.

When we are not enamored by the absolute holiness of God, we will not seek His glory. If God is "the man upstairs" or "my copilot," then He is really not any different from us. In reality, God is the self-existing Creator God, who breathed out the universe and all it contains and then fashioned it, creating all life-forms and humankind with less effort than we would spend blowing out a single candle. The holiness of God is absolute; He cannot be tempted with evil, and He Himself tempts no one (Jas 1:13). All we have ever seen and known is corruption. Thus, without becoming a student of the scriptures, we naturally have a low view of God. A low view of God does not lend itself to seeking His glory. To rightly understand His holiness is to tremble at the thought of it, to tremble in His presence as did Isaiah and the apostle John (Is 6:5; Rv 1:17). The greater our knowledge of His person, and His holiness, the greater our desire to honor and glorify Him. This is our obligation.

As we make progress in these steps of discipleship, we understand that being conformed to this world is to be stuck on ourselves; we are self-impressed. In the transformation that biblical discipleship requires, we must decrease, and He must increase. This will not happen unless we take every thought captive to make it obedient to Christ, to His purpose. We do not let a single thought escape our bodies until it is obedient to the purpose of Christ, and in doing that, we glorify God. When we develop a consistent habit of glorifying God in all that we say and do, a most wonderful thing happens. We look like the biblical Jesus to a watching world. This is the subject of the next chapter, step 5.

Study Questions

Time for some honesty. What is your view of God? Is He someone to meet on Sunday and then forget the rest of the week? Does your view of His holiness make you tremble?

How often do I say "I," "me," or "mine" to bring the focus of a conversation back to me?

How does what I am saying honor God?

Have I identified my spiritual gifts? Have I found someone or somewhere to serve in the body of Christ, the church?

CHAPTER 7

WORTHY OF THE GOSPEL

In diagram 1, step 5 states, "Your life should look like the biblical Jesus to the watching world." I base this on Philippians 1:27: "Only conduct yourselves in a manner worthy of the gospel of Christ." We learned in chapter 1 that as followers and disciples of Jesus Christ, we are not our own; we were bought at a price and belong to God (1 Cor 6:19–20). We are therefore morally obligated and duty bound to obey His commands and glorify Him in our bodies in all that we say and do. As we continue to mature in our personal discipleship more and more, our manner of life will be worthy of the gospel.

In chapter 2 we learned about the problem of worldliness in the church. All too often, the lives of those who attend church regularly do not look much different from those who don't. This is a failure of discipleship. Jesus is quoted in Luke 6:40 as saying, "A disciple is not above his teacher, but everyone when he is fully trained will be like his teacher." Over time, a person's life will resemble their "god." The book of Proverbs records the reflections of the Good Father in chapter 4: "I have taught you the way of wisdom; I have led you in the paths of uprightness" (Prv 4:11 ESV). There is something dreadfully wrong in the life of a person who claims to have been a Christian for some time, yet his or her life is still marked by the traits of the world. The apostle John wrote, "Do not love the world or the things in the world. If anyone loves the world, the love of the Father is not in him" (1 Jn 2:15). Worldliness and the church are mutually exclusive. They cannot coexist. Therefore, the worldly church is not of the Father.

The apostle Paul gave the church in Ephesus the same admonition that he gave to the Philippian church: "I therefore, a prisoner for the Lord, urge you to walk in a manner worthy of the calling to which you have been called" (Eph 4:1 ESV). And to the church in Colossae:

> And so, from the day we heard, we have not ceased to pray for you, asking that you may be filled with the knowledge of his will in all spiritual wisdom and understanding, so as to walk in a manner worthy of the Lord, fully pleasing to him, bearing fruit in every good work and increasing in the knowledge of God. (Col 1:9–10 ESV)

To the church in Thessalonica, he said,

> As you know, we treated each one of you as a father treats his own children, exhorting and encouraging you and insisting that you live in

a way worthy of God who calls you to his own
kingdom and his glory. (1 Thes 2:11–12)

To "walk in a manner worthy of the gospel of Christ," is
the normal, expected behavior of the disciple of Christ. Let's
look a little closer to better define what is expected. The Greek
word translated "only" in Philippians 1:27, *monon*, pronounced
mon'-on, is an adverb in the neuter form. It means "used to limit
or separate an action or state to the one designated in the verb
merely, only, alone."[1] The ISV of the Bible translates the word
only with the phrase "the only thing that matters." This word *only*
modifies the verb.

The ESV translates the verb in this verse (*politeuesthe*,
pronounced in its root form, *pol-it-yoo'-om-ahee*) as "your manner
of life." In the NKJV, it is "your conduct." Essentially, it means
to live as a citizen under the laws thereof. The word *let*, as in
step 3, Ephesians 4:29, has no corresponding word in the Greek,
but it is necessary in the English to convey the message, which
is that the action prescribed by the verb is under the control of
the individual: "Only let your manner of life." We are to focus
our energy, which is under our control, to conducting ourselves,
or to governing our behaviors in every event in our life in a way
consistent with a citizen of the kingdom of God, fully pleasing to
the King (Col 1:10).

The life worthy of the gospel of Christ is an intentional life.

---

[1] Walter Bauer, *A Greek-English Lexicon of the New Testament and Other Early
Christian Literature*, 2nd ed. Revised and Augmented by Wm. F. Arndt and F.
Wilbur Gingrich (Chicago: Univ. of Chicago Press) s.v. μονος.

Holiness is not the norm for fallen humanity, but it should be for the Christian. This is the passion for which Paul wishes to remain alive, the passion of holiness, which gives meaning to his life.

All events in our lives—at home, at work, at play—are to look like the *biblical* Jesus to a watching world. I emphasize "biblical" because having been in ministry for over thirty years, I know plenty of people whose idea of Jesus is anything but biblical. There are those who believe Jesus just loves and accepts everyone, but He had a pretty tough, unloving conversation with the religious leaders recorded in Matthew 23, where He pronounced seven woes against them. Why? Essentially because they were hypocrites who promoted a false gospel of faith-plus, faith plus works of the law. While He refused to condemn the woman taken in adultery (Jn 8:1–11), He condemned her sin while He rebuked her, saying, "Go, and sin no more" (Jn 8:11b NKJV). He did not condemn her because the Pharisees and scribes challenged Him with a question concerning the law (Jn 8:4–6a). According to the law, a person could only be convicted or condemned on the testimony of two or three eyewitnesses (Dt 17:6; 19:15), which Jesus was not. When the witnesses walked away, there was no one left who could condemn her—no eyewitnesses. Jesus never shrank away from calling sin what it is: sin. When Jesus confronted the rich young man regarding his slavish devotion to wealth, the man "went away sorrowful" (Mt 19:22). Jesus did not chase after him, begging him to come back. His love let him go to pursue his own destruction. The biblical Jesus expected humility and sincerity from the hypocrites, repentance from the sinners, and generous charity from the rich. Absent this, He allowed them to walk away.

To conduct our lives in a manner worthy of the gospel of Christ means we abide by the rules of heaven even when we are not in church. In all our conversations, we plan each word to edify the other person(s) at home, in our business relations, and in our leisure. We will govern our choice of clothes by the rules of heaven. Whether male or female, the command in 1 Peter 3:3–4 is appropriate:

> Let your beauty not be external—the braiding of hair and wearing of gold jewelry or fine clothes— but the inner person of the heart, the lasting beauty of a gentle and tranquil spirit, which is precious in God's sight.

An unhealthy devotion to external beauty is just as harmful to men as it is to women, especially when there is a corresponding neglect of developing the beauty of the character, the inner person. We should dress and adorn ourselves in such a way that does not draw attention to us (think clothes, hair, jewelry, tattoos, and so on). Drawing attention to ourselves, for whatever reason, glorifies us and, therefore, diminishes Christ, the exact opposite of our duty to Him: "He must become more important while I become less important" (Jn 3:30).

How we spend our money and use our resources reflect our God. As servants of the Messiah, we recognize that all we have is from Him, and that one day we will be accountable to Him for our use and disposition of all that He entrusted to us. Thus, it is very important that our priority, as Christians, is to live our lives in every detail within the parameters set out in the commands of Jesus—"teaching them to obey everything I have commanded you" (Mt 28:20a)—in a manner worthy of the gospel of Christ.

The apostle Paul wanted to know that the church was,

> standing firm in one spirit, with one mind, by
> contending side by side for the faith of the gospel,
> and by not being intimidated in any way by your
> opponents. This is a sign of their destruction, but
> of your salvation—a sign which is from God. (Phil
> 1:27b–28)

As disciples of the Master, we are to be one in spirit (similar views), and of one mind (similar passions); we are to be one in our understanding and in our will. Scholars are divided here whether "spirit" refers to the Spirit of God or the spirit of man. It makes little difference for, if in fact the disciple is true to God, then the Spirit of God is informing and controlling the spirit of man. This is the sense in this verse, according to *The Expositors Greek Testament*: "Here we are safe in holding that ἑνὶ πνεύματι [*heni pneumati*, one spirit] refers to the common, spiritual life implanted in them by the direct working of the Holy Spirit."[2] This world, with its passions and will, are in direct conflict with us. We are to contend (fight) together for personal and corporate holiness. We are not to be intimidated by the world: "the world is passing away with all its desires, but the person who does the will of God remains forever" (1 Jn 2:17). When the church tries to advance with rebellion in the ranks, there will be failure. Joshua and the army of Israel were initially defeated at Ai because of

---

[2] H.A.A. Kennedy, "Philippians," in *The Expositor's Greek Testament*, ed. W. Robertson Nicholl, (New York: George H. Doran Co., public domain), vol. 3.

rebellion in the ranks (Jo 7). It only took one rebellious man to cause the army of God to be defeated. Do not be that person!

In order for the church to look like the biblical Jesus to the watching world, we must present a united front. Every person, every individual believer/disciple must take their parts. As with a marching band, when even one person falls out of order, it skews the whole line. It is distorted, and we misrepresent Jesus.

Trying to decide on a movie? First ask, "What does holiness look like in this event?" Then begin at step 1: Do not conform, but be transformed by the renewing of your mind. Then continue with the remaining steps. Step 2: Take every thought captive, and make it obedient to Jesus. Step 3: Do not grieve the Holy Spirit of God. Step 4: Make certain your choice will honor and glorify God. Step 5: Choose so your life/choices will look like the biblical Jesus to a watching world.

Have a problem with alcohol or drugs? First ask, "What does holiness look like in this event?" Then begin following the steps. Struggle with pornography? Ask, "What does holiness look like in this event?" And begin the process. Continue this every day for every event. This is simple to learn though hard to do. But hard is not impossible.

When we learn this process and practice it, it will transform the church. We will transform our relationships. We could transform our work environments, at least our reactions to them. If we don't learn and practice it, the church will remain lethargic, anemic, and sick. There is a distorted and an inadequate representation of Jesus in the world because of the failure of the church to "make disciples, ... teaching them to obey everything I [Jesus] have commanded you."

Study Questions

This is a hard chapter. Take some time to reflect and talk to God about what your life looks like. Do you look like the biblical Jesus? In what areas do you struggle?

Choose one of your areas of struggle and work through the process here. Writing things down makes them concrete. Write your struggle and then go through every step of the process as demonstrated in this chapter. Then go to God in prayer and ask for His help as you commit to acting this out in your life.

Based on the evidence of my life, who is Jesus to me?

> In the beginning was the Word, and the Word was with God, and the Word was fully God. (Jn 1:1)

> Now the Word became flesh and took up residence among us. We saw his glory—the glory of the one and only, full of grace and truth, who came from the Father. (Jn 1:14)

CHAPTER 8

THE EXPRESSION

There is a principle in this model of discipleship that perhaps you have noticed by now. If not, allow me to point it out. If a person stumbles on any of the steps, it is because of a stumble on the previous step, and we can trace it all the way back to a stumble on the very first step. For example, let's say there is an event in a marriage; perhaps the husband speaks sharply to his wife. This is a stumble at step 3: "You are not permitted to say anything except that it edifies others" (Eph 4:29). This stumble results from a stumble on step 2 because the husband did not take every thought captive to make it obedient to Christ, which is a result from a stumble on step 1 because he reverted to being conformed to the pattern of this world (Rom 12:2). He responded from the world, not from the transformed life. The best way to proceed is to stop, reorganize, apologize, and start over at step 1 for this event. The husband, transformed by the renewing of his mind (step 1), would take every thought captive (step 2), design his remarks with the purpose to edify his wife (step 3), ask himself, "What does holiness look like?" (step 4), and based on that, pursue the discussion in a manner worthy of the gospel (step 5). Easy, right? Not for the proud, no. But in this, he would glorify God, which is the chief and highest end of humankind.

"Not for the proud." Pride has no place in the Christian life. "There are six things that the LORD hates, even seven things that are an abomination to him: haughty eyes, a lying tongue, and hands that shed innocent blood" (Prv 6:16–17). "Pride goes before destruction, and a haughty spirit before a fall. It is better to be lowly in spirit with the afflicted than to share the spoils with the proud" (Prv 16:18–19). "Before destruction the heart of a person is proud, but humility comes before honor" (Prv 18:12). "A proud and arrogant person, whose name is 'Scoffer,' acts with overbearing pride" (Prv 21:24). And from the NT, the unforgettable words of John the Baptizer: "He must become more important while I become less important" (Jn 3:30). Pride, or a haughty spirit is, at its root, idolatry. The proud person is in love with him- or herself and worships self. God does not tolerate such pride.

The Christian life is one of service to others. The proud person does not serve others; the proud person seeks to be served. The disciples James and John, the sons of Zebedee, desired honor in the kingdom by being seated on the left and the right hands of Jesus (Mk 10:35–40). Their mother even petitioned Jesus for this honor for her sons (Mt 20:20–21). This request, when it became known among the other disciples, caused a division in the camp. Pride does that; it causes division in the church and in personal relationships. The other disciples were angry, not because of some so-called righteous indignation, but because the presumptions of James and John and their mother infuriated their own pride. In this division, Jesus equated their attitudes with the attitude of a tyrant that we all hate but in some measure are. Then he said that the Son of Man did not come to be served but to serve! What King goes among His subjects seeking to serve others? King Jesus, that's who. What pastor, elder, or deacon goes through the congregation seeking whom he may serve? The biblical one, that's who. What husband comes home from work seeking to serve his wife and children? The biblical husband, that's who. The Christian life is a life of service to others.

I base step 1 on Romans 12:1–2. Now notice verse 3:

> For by the grace given to me I say to every one
> of you not to think more highly of yourself than
> you ought to think, but to think with sober
> discernment, as God has distributed to each of
> you a measure of faith. (Rom 12:3)

There are those who think more highly of themselves than they should; they think more highly of themselves than others think of them. On this verse, Albert Barnes comments,

> Not to over-estimate himself, or to think more
> of himself than he ought to. What is the true
> standard by which we ought to estimate ourselves
> he immediately adds. This is a caution against
> pride; and an exhortation not to judge of ourselves
> by our talents, wealth, or function, but to form

another standard of judging of ourselves, by our Christian character ... And the exhortation was that they should not judge of their own characters by the usual modes among people, but by their Christian attainments. There is no sin to which people are more prone than an inordinate self-valuation and pride. Instead of judging by what constitutes true excellence of character, they pride themselves on that which is of no intrinsic value; on rank, and titles, and external accomplishments; or on talents, learning, or wealth. The only true standard of character pertains to the principles of action, or to that which constitutes the moral nature of the man;[1]

The scriptures testify that we are all sinners (Jer 17:9; Rom 3:23; 1 Jn 1:8, 10). They command us to be transformed by the renewing of our minds (Rom 12:2). Jesus declared, "out of the abundance of the heart the mouth speaks" (Mt 12:34b ESV). Paul commanded,

Let the word of Christ dwell in you richly, teaching and exhorting one another with all wisdom, singing psalms, hymns, and spiritual songs, all with grace in your hearts to God. And whatever you do in word or deed, do it all in the

---

[1] Albert Barnes, *Notes on the Bible,* http://onlinebible.net, 2012.

name of the Lord Jesus, giving thanks to God the
Father through him. (Col 3:16–17)

A disciple mimics the life pattern of the Master. The disciple
of Christ memorizes scripture. If you memorize and practice the
five steps of discipleship with the associated scriptures, you will
notice a better reflection of Jesus Christ in your life. At each step
there are more scriptures than I have listed. Here are more for
steps 4 or 5:

> Do nothing from selfish ambition or conceit, but
> in humility count others more significant than
> yourselves. Let each of you look not only to his
> own interests, but also to the interests of others.
> (Phil 2:3–4 ESV)

I suggest that if you are not serving others in your Christian
life, you will stunt your discipleship. Can you name even one
person you are serving for his or her benefit, not your own? It
would be good to memorize and practice these verses. For good
measure.

The apostle Paul teaches the same doctrine of self-sacrificing
service to others in his letter to the Galatians:

> For in Christ Jesus neither circumcision nor
> uncircumcision carries any weight—the only
> thing that matters is faith working through love.
> (Gal 5:6)

> For you were called to freedom, brothers and
> sisters; only do not use your freedom as an
> opportunity to indulge your flesh, but through
> love serve one another. (Gal 5:13)

The churches in Galatia had been invaded by legalists promoting a works-based salvation. Rightly understood, the gospel of Jesus Christ frees us from the demands of legalism but promotes good works as evidence of salvation and transformation. To serve each other, to promote the welfare of the other, looks like the biblical Jesus to a watching world. When we serve each other, we demonstrate a regard for their edification and use the grace of God for His glory. John Calvin states,

> we have pointed out that liberty is one thing, and
> that the use of it is another thing. Liberty lies in
> the conscience, and looks to God; the use of it lies
> in outward matters, and deals not with God only,
> but with men.[2]

True Christian liberty finds its full expression in Christian service to others. God is not selfish. He wants us to be like Him, but all too often we want God to be like us. He is all about our best. And sadly, so are we.

The problem with legalism is that a person can dress up on

---

[2] John Calvin, *Calvin's Commentaries (Complete)*, trans. John King, Accordance electronic ed. (Edinburgh: Calvin Translation Society, 1847), paragraph 88287. https://accordance.bible/link/read/Calvin#88287

the outside without ever changing the inside. Jesus addressed this with some scribes and Pharisees:

> Woe to you, experts in the law and you Pharisees, hypocrites! You clean the outside of the cup and the dish, but inside they are full of greed and self-indulgence. Blind Pharisee! First clean the inside of the cup, so that the outside may become clean too!
>
> Woe to you, experts in the law and you Pharisees, hypocrites! You are like whitewashed tombs that look beautiful on the outside but inside are full of the bones of the dead and of everything unclean. In the same way, on the outside you look righteous to people, but inside you are full of hypocrisy and lawlessness. (Mt 23:25–28)

Personality can fake Christian service for a season, a short season, but character isn't as easy to fake. Eventually, our behaviors will emulate our characters. Discipleship seeks to transform the character until it's clean on the inside, producing clean on the outside.

The true measure of a disciple of Christ is character, piety: "A disciple is not greater than his teacher, but everyone when fully trained will be like his teacher" (Lk 6:40). Our goal as disciples of Christ is to look like the biblical Jesus to a watching world. Pride will never permit that. We must develop an honest appraisal of ourselves based on our Christian piety, our Christian character.

It is the will of God for your life that you walk in accordance to His statutes and that you do the hard work of discipleship—the development of a Christian character. The will of God and the power of God can bring this to fruition:

> So then, my dear friends, just as you have always
> obeyed, not only in my presence but even more in
> my absence, continue working out your salvation
> with awe and reverence, for the one bringing forth
> in you both the desire and the effort—for the sake
> of his good pleasure—is God. (Phil 2:12–13)

The Lord God promised through the prophet Ezekiel in the new covenant,

> I will give you a new heart, and I will put a new
> spirit within you. I will remove the heart of stone
> from your body and give you a heart of flesh.
> I will put my Spirit within you; I will take the
> initiative and you will obey my statutes and
> carefully observe my regulations. (Ez 36:26–27)

The late Dr. R. C. Sproul, in his book *Renewing Your Mind,* wrote, "Our effectiveness as Christians, our strength as a church, are inseparably related to our intimacy with the Spirit of God."[3] We cannot transform the character through legalism, only by a close, intimate working of the Holy Spirit with a person. We develop the picture-perfect character in the dark room of prayer

---

[3] R. C. Sproul, *Renewing Your Mind.* (Ada, MI: Baker Books, 1998), 169.

and submission. We must submit to the Word of God, and learn through repetition to do the commands of the gospel. Dr. Sinclair Ferguson wrote,

> The transformation of our lives takes place through the renewal of our minds: right thinking about the truth of the gospel motivates right living in the power of the gospel. (Rom 12:1–2).[4]

Throughout this book, I have stressed the difficulty of the task before us, to remake our character in order to reflect the biblical Jesus to a watching world. And to be sure, it is difficult. It requires the utmost diligence. But difficult is not impossible. This transformation is made possible *only* in the power of the Holy Spirit of God. Peter prayed, "May grace and peace be lavished on you as you grow in the rich knowledge of God and of Jesus our Lord!" (2 Pt 1:2) "As you grow." Philippians 2:13 (ESV) says, "It is God who works in you, both to will and to work for his good pleasure." We must participate in our rescue, but it is God who *causes* the growth, the increase (1 Cor 3:6–9). Do not grieve the Holy Spirit, but do not underestimate Him either. His will is your sanctification. You have been appointed for holiness.

The diligence of discipleship—the potential to release the power of God in your life, in your relationships, in your church, and in the church. The diligence of discipleship is a paradigm-shifting idea. Once you embrace it, your life will truly never be

---

[4] Sinclair B. Ferguson, *By Grace Alone: How the Grace of God Amazes Me.* (Sanford, FL: Reformation Trust Publishing, 2010), 105.

the same. The Holy Spirit will work on you and in you. Be honest with God as you embark on this journey. The truth of the gospel is that Jesus is the Messiah, the Son of the Living God (Mt 16:16). He builds His church on that doctrine, and when the disciples of Jesus are faithful to His commands, the gates of hell shall not prevail (Mt 16:18), not in your life and not in the church. Our Lord bless you!

Diagram 1: Steps to Success
The Process of Discipleship

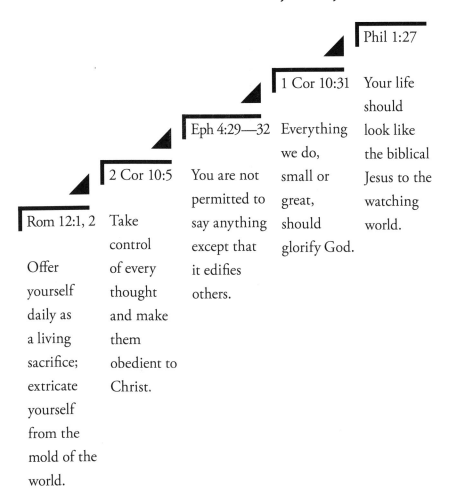

Phil 1:27

1 Cor 10:31 Your life should look like the biblical Jesus to the watching world.

Eph 4:29—32 Everything we do, small or great, should glorify God.

2 Cor 10:5 You are not permitted to say anything except that it edifies others.

Rom 12:1, 2 Take control of every thought and make them obedient to Christ.

Offer yourself daily as a living sacrifice; extricate yourself from the mold of the world.

---

1. Remember the sticker on your mirror: You might be looking at the problem.
2. You must participate in your own rescue; "make every effort" (2 Pt 1:5–8).